1

All contents of the book are the exclusive property
of Stefano Benedetti. Marketing ban, even partially.

Index

Introduction

This book aims those people that want to know about the market valuation of a vintage or antique camera to buy or sell.

The cameras produced produced by more than a century and a half are countless and most of a particular interest for the collector, the amateur photographer, the antique dealer and retailer of photographic equipment.

Tens of millions of estimates from Italy, from Europe and America have been examined.

The evaluations of each model were then processed by computer to finally establish a reliable estimate range.

The camera prices in this book are not the major or minor price, but an average price among most reliable.

About the provided values, the oscillation is low, if the device is within the conservation standards.

In fact, all these assessments are referred to a functional unit, in good condition, equipped with standard optical series, provided in the fabrication period.

Standard optical means, for example, a lens of focal length of 50 mm on a frame 24X36 mm. Obviously the standard for larger or smaller film sizes will be a more or less large focal of 50 mm. The problem there isn't for cameras with fixing optical, while it is present for the so-called optical benches, units with at least a chassis and standard optics.

Functional unit means a camera whose shutter operates as well as the aperture and the exposure system and tape drive, if present. Also optics must not show any serious abrasions or imperfections.

Obviously it does not mean that the unit is immaculate, but that nevertheless, considered the age that has, it is still working with the body not excessively deteriorated.

The index of this book is ordered alphabetically by manufacturer name.

Sometimes the name of a person, rather than a brand is reported, this is due to productions by craftsmen of the past. Names replicated along with others, are attributable to mergers or agreements among more factories.

For each manufacturer, there is a table, accessible from the index directly.

The first column is the name of the camera model or elements to identify it are reported. The second column defines the year of production. If it is not shown, it means that the estimate is independent from the year of commercialization. The third column shows the minimum and maximum value as averages of the values found during the search. The prices are expressed in Euro.

If near the year symbol * is present, it means the price is inferred, but not certain. If near to the symbol euro in the assessment the * symbol is present, it means that the estimate is very likely to change. This happens for cameras for with an offer high price. In this case if you are buying or selling just that device, be very careful.

Buying Guide

Primarily focus on price. Bid too low could hide some defects that cannot be found with a superficial examination. We have not taken account these offers in the prices computation. To better understand it follows a consideration.

For a camera model we found that oscillated between 60 and 80 €. Then we found one that was less than 2 €!

Obviously we could not think that all the other sellers were dishonest, but that offer was hiding something.

Similarly a too high price, compared to all other, is obviously an attempt to achieve an excessive gain.

Mechanical cameras

To determine the conservation status of a camera begin to run these tests on cameras that allow them.

1) Examine the camera body. Can be tolerated abrasion and scratches due to the use over the years, but the camera body must not be damaged or deformed.

2) Open the film compartment. Examine the mechanisms and dragging housing that have to be in good condition. For example, if present a winding reel with teeth, see if these are too worn or damaged.

3) By keeping open the machine back, try to charge the shutter. Then try to take a picture and observe if from behind the shutter behaves in a consonant manner.

4) If your camera has a shutter with the curtains, make sure they are not worn or damaged. Also be sure that after shooting the curtains do not let that the light leak out.

5) Examine the bottom of the camera. Dents on the bottom could indicate suffered violent collisions.

6) If the machine has a pentaprism at the top, check that has not been damaged and that the eyed vision is clear and clean.

7) If the machine has interchangeable lens, remove the lens and check that the light transmission system is intact and no fogging or stains.

8) If the machine is of the SLR Vision type, check that the broadcast mirror is intact and clean and take care also of the cushioning pads on which the mirror is placed while shooting.

9) Shoot with selector all times of the camera, if any. While you are shooting, if your camera allows, hold open the back and set some diaphragm aperture values. Notìce that the blades close properly and that there is no unusual noise when you are shooting. Try to set the time interval (16-8-4-2-1 sec. and so on) in order to establish if the shutter mechanism is quite distorted. If the camera has B or T lay, check them. By setting B lay the shutter must remain open as long as you hold down the button. By setting T lay the shutter must remain open, after that you have pressed the button, and closed when it is pressed again.

The best way to determine the proper operation of a camera is taking a series of photos before buying it.

This possibility depends on the seller who is not always willing.

If you can take pictures, do the following. Of course, in this text you find all kinds of shots you have to do, but this depends on the characteristics of the machine. Take all those that technically the camera is able to achieve.

1) Check the flash sync works. If there is the housing slide or the flash is mounted with a connector, shoot with times of 1/60, 1/125, 1/250 and aperture all combinations. Many machines have indicated the flash sync time on the selector, in this case carried out only a series of photos.

2) Place three pencils at different distances; the first at 2 meters, the second at 4 meters, the third at 6 meters. Take a series of photographs with different aperture, focusing on the first, the second and the third pencil.

3) Verify that the machine meter operates correctly. Take a photo of the ISO sensitivity as shown by the film. Then take again with the same time provided by the meter, but set the diaphragms with 4 more open values and then up to 4 more closed values. Once printed the photos, that made with the meter value must be that exact.

4) If it is a machine with electrical or electronic motor, make sure that you drag the film properly. If the drive is manual, place a black cap on the lens, load and shoot until the end of the film. Rewind the film until you hear the click of the film tail that comes out from the spool. Retrieve the film and mount it again.

5) Check the machine long time. Set the shutter speed of at ½ sec ,1 se,c 2 sec, 4 sec, 8 sec and so on. Get with the exposure meter the right value of the diaphragm at different settings. The scene must be always the same. Then place the camera on a tripod, so that the scene is always the same. The resulting prints have to be equal. The same test can also be applied for shutter shorter times.

In general, any photos you do with any camera, the resulting prints must not show halos, stains, blurs, lines, or other anomalies. Moreover, if the lens that you have used is standard, there must be no excessive distortion or random focus plans different from those that you wanted to get in the film.

Identification of camera parts

It follows a brief guide to identify the elements of the most popular cameras in the twentieth century. No report in this book all types of cameras, will illustrate only the two most popular types in the twentieth century: the 35 mm SLR cameras and TLR cameras.

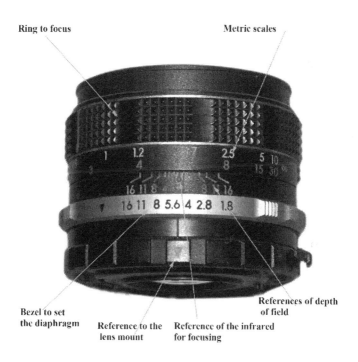

Ring to focus

Metric scales

Bezel to set
the diaphragm

Reference to the
lens mount

Reference of the infrared
for focusing

References of depth
of field

Reference of photographic lens locking

Pentaprism camera

Self-timer

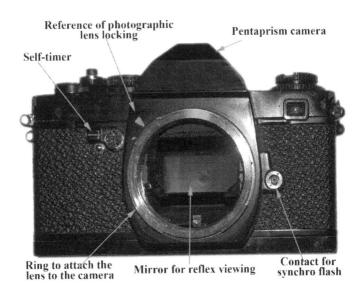

Ring to attach the lens to the camera

Mirror for reflex viewing

Contact for synchro flash

Reference of the film plane

Shutter release button

Counting frame

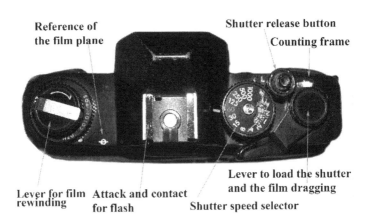

Lever for film rewinding

Attack and contact for flash

Lever to load the shutter and the film dragging

Shutter speed selector

20

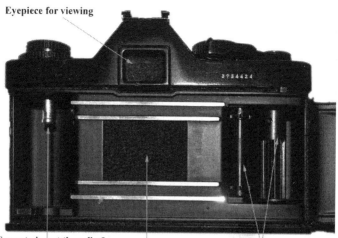

Eyepiece for viewing

Space to insert the roll of film and spool for dragging

Plane shutter

Space and reels for the dragging and winding the film

Removable lens to magnify the scene

Reclosable system for the vision and the focus

Frosted glass on which the scene appears

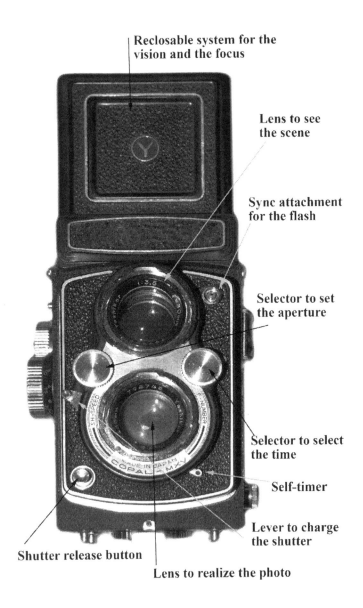

Reclosable system for the
vision and the focus

Lens to see
the scene

Sync attachment
for the flash

Selector to set
the aperture

Selector to select
the time

Self-timer

Lever to charge
the shutter

Shutter release button

Lens to realize the photo

Reclosable system
to see the scene

Lens to magnify
the scene

Selector for the
film speed

Scale for depth of field   Knob to focus

Estimates

Agfa

Manufacturer-model	Year	€
Agfa Agfamatic 100 Sensor	1970	35-45
Agfa Agfamatic 126	----	25-40
Agfa Agfamatic 200 Sensor	----	25-40
Agfa Agfamatic 50	1972	30-50
Agfa Agfamatic 508 Pocket	----	30-50
Agfa Agfamatic 901 E Plus	----	25-40
Agfa Ambi Silette	----	75-90
Agfa Ambiflex I	1959	70-120
Agfa Ambiflex II	1960	70-120
Agfa Ambiflex III	1962	110-
Agfa Ansco	----	40-60
Agfa Ansco P16	----	25-40
Agfa Bilinar Enamel	----	50-70
Agfa Billy Clack	----	40-55
Agfa Captain	----	15-28
Agfa Clack	1954	45-60
Agfa Clipper PD16	1930	50-70
Agfa Colorflex	----	90-115
Agfa Isola	----	25-35
Agfa Isolette I	----	40-60
Agfa Isolette II	----	70-90
Agfa Isolette III	----	128-
Agfa Isolette L	----	120-
Agfa Isolette Rangefinder	----	90-110
Agfa Isoly I	1961	25-40

Manufacturer-model	Year	€
Agfa Isopack 126	----	30-50
Agfa IsoRapid	----	25-40
Agfa JGenar	1953	250-300
Agfa JSorette	----	25-40
Agfa Karat 36	----	190-240
Agfa Karat IV	----	200-240
Agfa Movex Automatic II	1963	30-50
Agfa Optima 1035 Sensor	----	70-90
Agfa Optima 1535	----	100-140
Agfa Optima 200	----	25-40
Agfa Optima 500 Sensor	1969	30-50
Agfa Optima I	1960	25-40
Agfa Optima II	----	35-55
Agfa Optima II S	----	20-30
Agfa Optima Rapid 250 V	1966	40-60
Agfa Optima Reflex	----	170-230
Agfa Parat I	----	35-60
Agfa Rangefinder	----	15-25
Agfa Record II	----	70-90
Agfa Record II Billy Prontor	----	100-140
Agfa Reflex	1961	120-180
Agfa Selectaflex I	1963	70-110
Agfa Selectaflex II	1963	190-130
Agfa Selectra Prontor matic p	----	30-50
Agfa Selectronic 1	1980	55-85

Manufacturer-model	Year	€
Agfa Selectronic 2	1980	90-130
Agfa Selectronic 3	1980	120-160
Agfa Silette F	1966	50-70
Agfa Silette L	----	30-50
Agfa Silette L type 2	1958	30-50
Agfa Silette Rapid F	----	18-28
Agfa Syncro Box	----	30-45
Agfa Trophy	1944	40-65
Agfa Viking Pb20	----	60-90
Agfa X 126	----	30-45

Agilux

Manufacturer-model	Year	€
Agilux Agiflash	----	40-50
Agilux Agiflex	----	20-35
Agilux Agiflex III	----	55-75
Agilux Agifold	----	80-100
Agilux Agifold II	----	120-160
Agilux Agimatic	----	100-140
Agilux Colt 44	----	40-60

Aires

Manufacturer-model	Year	€
Aires 35 II	----	40-55
Aires 35 III	1956	80
Aires 35 III C	----	
Aires 35 III L	----	80
Aires 35- V	----	150-190
Aires Penta 35	1960	70
Aires Viscount	----	45
Airesflex II	----	70

Alba

Manufacturer-model	Year	€
Alba Gamma	----	40-55
Alba Regno	1900 *	180-220

Albinar

Manufacturer-model	Year	€
Albinar Ms-2 Black	----	40-60

Alpa

Manufacturer-model	Year	€
Alpa 10 D	1968	700-900
Alpa 10 D gold	1968	1500-2500
Alpa 10 s	----	1400-1700
Alpa 10 S	1972	1200-1600
Alpa 10d	----	800-1000
Alpa 11 E	1970	2400-3200
Alpa 11 SI	1976	450-550
Alpa 11a	----	300-400
Alpa 11e	----	1200-1400
Alpa 11E black	1970	900-1100
Alpa 11EL	1972	1000-1400
Alpa 11SI	1976	1800-2200
Alpa 3C	----	350-450
Alpa 4	1952	800-1000
Alpa 5	1952	800-900
Alpa 6	1957	550-650
Alpa 6 C	1956	550-650
Alpa 6b	----	800-1000
Alpa 7	1952	350-450
Alpa 7 S	1958	350-450
Alpa 8 B	1965	600-700
Alpa 9 D	1968	600-700
Alpa 9 F	1965	1000-1400

Manufacturer-model	Year	€
Alpa Alnea 7	----	600-700
Alpa Bolca I	1942	1000-2000
Alpa I Reflex	1944	1600-2000
Alpa II Reflex	1945	500-700
Alpa III Reflex	1949	1200-1600
Alpa SI 2000	1977	250-350
Alpa SI 2000	1978	95-120
Alpa SI 3000	1980	200-300
Alpa SI 3000 S	1982	250-350

Altissa

Manufacturer-model	Year	€
Altissa Altissar Periskop	----	40-50
Altissa Altix IV	----	80-100
Altissa Altix N	1967	40-55
Altissa Altix V	----	120-170
Altissa Altix V arancione	----	160-200
Altissa box	----	30-50
Altissa Eho	----	65-85

Argus

Manufacturer-model	Year	€
Argus 260 Automatic	----	18-30
Argus 40	----	18-30
Argus 520	----	18-30
Argus 75	----	25-40
Argus A	----	18-28
Argus A2b	----	18-30
Argus A-5	----	18-30
Argus A-Four	----	20-35
Argus Argoflex	1940	15-25
Argus Argoflex 75	----	20-35
Argus Argoflex Seventy-Five	----	18-30
Argus Autronic	----	15-25
Argus C3	----	18-25
Argus C3 Colormatic	1960	18-28
Argus C33	----	75-95
Argus C4	----	28-40
Argus C44R	----	90-140
Argus CC Color	----	35-55
Argus Cintar	----	15-25
Argus Dx Panorama	----	18-25
Argus Ilex	----	40-60
Argus Instant Load 284	----	18-28
Argus Irc A2B	1947	18-28
Argus Irc A2f	----	18-28
Argus Kamera	----	45-55
Argus STL 1000	----	25-45

Asahai Pentax

Manufacturer-model	Year	€
Asahi P Spotmatic	1964	100-140
Asahi Pentax	1957	300-400
Asahi Pentax 645	1984	28-450
Asahi Pentax 645 N	1998	260-300
Asahi Pentax 645 N II	1998	280-340
Asahi Pentax 67	1990	120-170
Asahi Pentax 67 II	1998	1000-1400
Asahi Pentax 6X7	1969	340-420
Asahi Pentax A3	1985	25-40
Asahi Pentax AP	----	170-200
Asahi Pentax auto 110	----	30-50
Asahi Pentax Auto Spy	----	28-40
Asahi Pentax ES	1972	120-170
Asahi Pentax ES II	1973	100-140
Asahi Pentax ES II MD	1975	170-220
Asahi Pentax IST	2003	50-70
Asahi Pentax K	1958	128-145
Asahi Pentax K, nera	1958	300-400
Asahi Pentax K1000	1977	80-120
Asahi Pentax K1000	1994	170-320
Asahi Pentax K2	1975	60-80
Asahi Pentax K2 DMD	1976	170-240

Manufacturer-model	Year	€
Asahi Pentax K2, black	1975	210
Asahi Pentax KM	1975	80-140
Asahi Pentax KM, MD	1975	200-240
Asahi Pentax KX	1975	60-80
Asahi Pentax KX MD	1975	320-380
Asahi Pentax LX	1980	320-370
Asahi Pentax LX oro	1980	2600-3000
Asahi Pentax ME	1976	45-65
Asahi Pentax ME Super	1980	90-120
Asahi Pentax ME-F	1981	90-140
Asahi Pentax MG	1982	28-45
Asahi Pentax MV	1980	28-45
Asahi Pentax MV-1	1980	40-60
Asahi Pentax MX	1976	180-220
Asahi Pentax MZ-10	1996	28-45
Asahi Pentax MZ-3	1997	70-90
Asahi Pentax MZ-30	2000	28-45
Asahi Pentax MZ-5	1996	28-45
Asahi Pentax MZ-50	1997	28-45
Asahi Pentax MZ-5N	1996	28-45
Asahi Pentax MZ-6	2001	50-70
Asahi Pentax MZ-60	2001	28-45
Asahi Pentax MZ-7	1999	25-40
Asahi Pentax MZ-M	1997	28-45
Asahi Pentax MZ-S	2001	160-200

Manufacturer-model	Year	€
Asahi Pentax P30	1985	28-45
Asahi Pentax P30N	1989	25-40
Asahi Pentax P30T	1991	25-40
Asahi Pentax P50	1986	28-45
Asahi Pentax Program A	1984	25-40
Asahi Pentax S	1957	80-100
Asahi Pentax S1A	1963	40-60
Asahi Pentax S3	1961	40-60
Asahi Pentax SF10	----	40-60
Asahi Pentax SF7	1988	28-45
Asahi Pentax SFX	1987	25-40
Asahi Pentax SFX N	1988	25-40
Asahi Pentax SL	1968	90-130
Asahi Pentax SP 1000	1973	70-90
Asahi Pentax SP 500	1971	50-70
Asahi Pentax SP II	1971	80-120
Asahi Pentax SPF	1973	120-170
Asahi Pentax Spotmatic F	1973	260-300
Asahi Pentax Spotmatic II	1971	240-320
Asahi Pentax Spotmatic MD	1964	325-400
Asahi Pentax Spotmatic SP	1964	120-170
Asahi Pentax Super A	1983	40-60

Manufacturer-model	Year	€
Asahi Pentax SV	1962	90-130
Asahi Pentax SV, black	1962	90-120
Asahi Pentax Z-1	1992	140-180
Asahi Pentax Z-10	1991	25-40
Asahi Pentax Z-1P	1994	180-220
Asahi Pentax Z-20	1992	25-40
Asahi Pentax Z-50P	1993	25-40
Asahi Pentax Z-70, Z-70P	1994	25-40
Asahi Pentax, black	----	1800-2200
Asahiflex I	1952	450-550
Asahiflex I a	1953	200-240
Asahiflex II a	1955	270-310
Asahiflex II b	1954	300-400

Baby

Manufacturer-model	Year	€
Baby 4X4, gray	1957	200-220
Baby 4X4, original	1931	500-550

Balda

Manufacturer-model	Year	€
Baby Jubilette	----	80-100
Balda	1936	55-70
Balda Baldamatic II	----	45-60
Balda Baldax	1930	55-70
Balda Baldessa Ib	----	40-60
Balda Baldessamat-Rf	----	28-40
Balda Baldina	1954	40-55
Balda Baldinette	----	60-75
Balda Baldix	----	80-100
Balda CE 35	----	60-80
Balda Juwella	1936	70-90
Balda Microscope Camera	----	60-75
Balda Pontina	----	40-60
Balda Rival	----	20-35
Balda Springbox	1933	110-140
Balda Super Baldinette	----	150-200

Balola

Manufacturer-model	Year	€
Balola	----	50-70

Beauty

Manufacturer-model	Year	€
Beauty Lite III	----	55
Beauty LM	----	40

Beier

Manufacturer-model	Year	€
Beier Beier-Flex	----	500
Beier Beirette Vsn	----	80-120
Beier Beirette	1963	25-40
Beier Beirax,		30-45
Beier Beirette V		20-35
Beier Precisa Binor		60-85
Beier Rifax	1936	180-250

Bell&Howell

Manufacturer-model	Year	€
Bell & Howell Auto 35	1969	30-50
Bell & Howell BF705	----	18-28
Bell & Howell Focus Free	----	25-40
Bell & Howell Foton	----	140-180
Bell & Howell Tdc Stereo	----	80-100

Bencini

Manufacturer-model	Year	€
Bencini	1939-1949 *	34-44
Bencini	1972-1979	18-25
Bencini	1978-1979	24-34
Bencini Argo	1970-1971	24-34
Bencini Bencini Koroll 24	1979-1984	24-34
Bencini Comet	1973-1978	24-34
Bencini Comet 100	1975-1985	22-29
Bencini Comet 118s	1937-1939 *	35-45
Bencini Comet 126x	1984-1989	34-44
Bencini Comet 126xl	1953-1955	45-55
Bencini Comet 200	1979-1989	22-29
Bencini Comet 200x	1976-1979	34-44
Bencini Comet 218	1975-1979	45-55
Bencini Comet 218s	1976-1979	45-55
Bencini Comet 226xl	1972-1975	22-29
Bencini Comet 235	----	35-45
Bencini Comet 3	1973-1985	22-29
Bencini Comet 318	1978-1989	22-29
Bencini Comet 318s	----	34-44
Bencini Comet 326xl	1966-1971	34-44
Bencini Comet 335	1981-1989	34-44
Bencini Comet 335	----	90-100

Manufacturer-model	Year	€
Bencini Comet 335	1963-1973	22-30
Bencini Comet 35	1962-1972	22-30
Bencini Comet 35	1979-1984	80-90
Bencini Comet 36	1959-1973	34-44
Bencini Comet 4	1963-1973	34-44
Bencini Comet 4	1985-1989	60-70
Bencini Comet 400	1937 1939 *	35-45
Bencini Comet 404	1974-1979	34-44
Bencini Comet 404x	1945-1952 *	90-100
Bencini Comet 418	1961-1970	34-44
Bencini Comet 418s	1979-1984	34-44
Bencini Comet 435 Elect.	1971-1977	34-44
Bencini Comet 44	1957-1960	24-34
Bencini Comet 455x	1948-1955	45-55
Bencini Comet 455xl	1965-1972	60-70
Bencini Comet 505x	1974-1979	34-44
Bencini Comet 535	1963-1972	150
Bencini Comet 555x	1955-1970	34-44
Bencini Comet 600xl	1955-1959	80-90
Bencini Comet 635	1958-1960	118-128
Bencini Comet 800xl	1937-1939 *	80-90
Bencini Comet II	1979-1984	15-25
Bencini Comet II	1985-1989	55-65
Bencini Comet II Sincro	1955-1963	34-44

Manufacturer-model	Year	€
Bencini Comet III	1960-1962	24-34
Bencini Comet K 35	1969-1972	55-70
Bencini Comet Nk 135	1970-1971	24-34
Bencini Comet Nk 135	1976-1979	34-44
Bencini Comet Nuova	1963-1973	18-28
Bencini Comet Rapid	1965-1972	60-70
Bencini Comet Rapid	1969-1971	22-30
Bencini Comet S	1980-1989	34-44
Bencini Cometa	1956-1969	45-55
Bencini Deko	1946-1951	85-95
Bencini Delta	1980-1989	34-44
Bencini Erno	1945-1947 *	90-100
Bencini Etna	1963-1973 *	34-44
Bencini Gabry	1940-1957 *	60-70
Bencini Koroll	1979-1984	34-44
Bencini Koroll 2	1951-1955	34-44
Bencini Koroll 2	1972-1975	18-28
Bencini Koroll 24	1976-1979	50-60
Bencini Koroll 24s	1969-1970	24-34
Bencini Koroll 35	1959-1960	75-85
Bencini Koroll CMF	----	45-65
Bencini Koroll Marine	1979-1984	34-44
Bencini Koroll S	1951-1955	75-85
Bencini Korollette	1979-1984	34-44

Manufacturer-model	Year	€
Bencini Personal 35	1970-1977	34-44
Bencini Personal Reporter	1979-1984	34-44
Bencini Relex	1979-1984	34-44
Bencini Relex II	1940-1942 *	75-85
Bencini Relex S	1955-1974	34-44
Bencini Robi	1975-1979	34-44
Bencini Roby	1979-1984	34-44
Bencini Rolet	1979-1984	24-34
Bencini Unimatic 600	1970-1971	100-120
Bencini Unimatic 800	1966-1971	34-44
Bencini Unimatic 808	1970-1971	34-44

Blair

Manufacturer-model	Year	€
Blair 5X7, Model 2	----	600-800
Blair No. 3a Folding Model	----	95-120
Blair No.1 Hawk-Eye 4"x5"	1893-1898	400-500
BLAIR Weno Red	1896-1900	250-320
BlairNO. 3 Folding	----	120-170

Bolsey

Manufacturer-model	Year	€
Bolsey 35 Model B	----	40-60
Bolsey B2	----	70-80
Bolsey Camera PH-324A	----	450-550
Bolsey Gauthie	1949	50-70
Bolsey Jubilee	1955	150-180

Bower

Manufacturer-model	Year	€
Bower Bower-X	----	55

Braun

Manufacturer-model	Year	€
Braun Bravo	----	20-35
Braun Nurmberg C-35	----	25-40
Braun Nurmberg Norca	----	70-90
Braun Paxette Panto	----	60-80
Braun Super Colorette	1956-1958	45-60
Nurnberg Paxette	----	25-40

Burke&James

Manufacturer-model	Year	€
Burke & James 4x5 Press	1945*	170-200
Burke & James B & J Press	----	200-220
Burke & James Monorail	----	400-500
Burke & James Press Camera	----	400-450
Burke & James Watson	----	150-170
Camera 8x10	----	250-350
Ingento Model 2	----	200-250
Rembrandt Camera Model 1	----	140-160

Calumet

Manufacturer-model	Year	€
Calumet 4x5 Monorail	----	200-250
Calumet Cambo 4x5 Monorail	----	380-420

Calypso

Manufacturer-model	Year	€
CalypsoPhot	1960	450-500

Canon

Manufacturer-model	Year	€
Canon 7	1963	120-1700
Canon 7 nera	1961	800-1000
Canon 7S	1965	700-900
Canon 7S nera	1965	250-350
Canon A-1	1978	90-130
Canon AE-1	1976	80-100
Canon AE-1 Program	1981	120-160
Canon AE-1 Program, nera	1981	190-230
Canon AL 1	1982	65-80
Canon AL-1 black	1982	80-100
Canon AT 1	1977	65-80
Canon AT-1, black	1977	80-100
Canon Autoboy Jet	----	65-80
Canon AV-1	1979	55-65
Canon Canonet	----	70-90
Canon Canonet G-III QL17	----	55-75
Canon EF	1974	100-140
Canon EF-M	1991	80-100
Canon EOS 1	1989	130-170
Canon EOS 1 N	1994	180-220
Canon EOS 1 N RS	1999	350-450
Canon EOS 1 V	----	350-450
Canon EOS 10	1990	140-180
Canon EOS 100	1991	80-100

Manufacturer-model	Year	€
Canon EOS 1000	1990	65-80
Canon EOS 1000 F	1991	65-80
Canon EOS 1000 FN	1992	70-90
Canon EOS 1000 N	1992	70-90
Canon EOS 3	1998	300-350
Canon EOS 30	2000	55-65
Canon EOS 30 date	2000	120-160
Canon EOS 30 V	2004	40-60
Canon EOS 300	1999	70-90
Canon EOS 300 V	2002	55-65
Canon EOS 3000	1999	70-90
Canon EOS 3000 V	2003	30-50
Canon EOS 300X	2004	55-65
Canon EOS 33	2000	55-65
Canon EOS 33 V	2000	120-170
Canon EOS 5	1992	260-300
Canon EOS 50	1995	80-120
Canon EOS 50 E	1995	80-120
Canon EOS 500	1993	80-120
Canon EOS 500 N	1996	65-80
Canon EOS 5000	1995	65-80
Canon EOS 50E	1995	45-65
Canon EOS 55 back datary	2001	130
Canon EOS 600	1989	70-90

Manufacturer-model	Year	€
Canon EOS 620	1987	65-80
Canon EOS 630	2001	70-90
Canon EOS 650	1987	80-100
Canon EOS 700	1990	45-60
Canon EOS 750	1988	45-60
Canon EOS 850	1988	45-60
Canon EOS IX (Aps)	1996	90-130
Canon EOS IX-7 (Aps)	1998	45-60
Canon EOS RT	1989	100-140
Canon EX-EE	1968	90-130
Canon EXEE QL	1968	80-100
Canon F1	1971	180-220
Canon F1 (n)	1976	320-370
Canon F1 (n) Olympics	1980	400-500
Canon F1 High Speed	1971	2000-2600
Canon F1 New	1981	240-300
Canon F1 New AE	1981	320-370
Canon FP	1964	80-100
Canon FT	1966	55-65
Canon FT Chrome	----	55-70
Canon FT QL	1966	90-130
Canon FTb	1971	70-90
Canon FTb (n) QL	1974	45-60
Canon FTb QL	1971	25-40

Manufacturer-model	Year	€
Canon FX	1964	65-80
Canon Hansa	1937	6000-8000*
Canon Hansa NK	1936	9000-11000*
Canon II b	1952	900-1100
Canon II d2	----	60-85
Canon IIF	1950	450-550
Canon III	1951	180-220
Canon IV	1951	350-420
Canon IV Sb	1952	90-150
Canon IV Sb2	1952	500-600
Canon Ivsb	----	220-270
Canon J	1939	4000-6000
Canon J II	1946	2500-3500
Canon JS	1939	4000-6000*
Canon L1	1956	1500-2200
Canon MC Autofocus	----	95-140
Canon NS	1939	2500-3500
Canon Pellix	1963	55-65
Canon Pellix QL	1965	90-130
Canon S	1939	2200-2700
Canon S-II	1947	350-450
Canon Sure Shot 76	----	50-65
Canon T 50	1983	35-50
Canon T 60	1990	40-60

Manufacturer-model	Year	€
Canon T 70	1984	70-90
Canon T 80	1985	55-65
Canon T 90	1986	100-140
Canon TLb QL	1973	25-40
Canon Tx	----	50-65
Canon VI-L	1958	520-570
Canon VT	1956	250-310
Canonex	1963	90-120
Canonflex	1959	120-160
Canonflex R 2000	1960	130-170
Canonflex RM	1962	110-140
Canonflex RM Nera	1962	550-650

Carena

Manufacturer-model	Year	€
Carena 35EE	----	30-45
Carena Computer E	1975	50-60
Carena CX-500	----	45-55
Carena K-SM1	1979	50-60
Carena RS	----	25-30
Carena RSD	1977	30-50
Carena SEL 2	1976	30-50
Carena SLF 2	1977	40-60
Carena SLR 1000	1976	30-50
Carena SRH 1001	1977	30-50
Carena SRH 760	----	30-50

Certo

Manufacturer-model	Year	€
Certo Certofix	----	70-90
Certo Certonet 0	----	40
Certo Certosport	----	140-180
CERTO Dollina	----	120-140
Certo Dollina 11	----	70-90
Certo KN35	----	20-40
Certo Phot	----	20-35
Certo Six 6	----	50-70
Certo SL 110	----	18-25
Certo Super Dolina II	----	80

Chinon

Manufacturer-model	Year	€
Chinon 35 FA	----	45-65
Chinon 358RZ	----	18-28
Chinon 35F-EE	----	55-65
Chinon 35FX-III	----	30-50
Chinon Auto 386Z	----	15-20
Chinon Auto 6001		20-40
Chinon Auto GL	----	18-25

Manufacturer-model	Year	€
Chinon CA 4	1980	40-60
Chinon CE 2	1976	35-45
Chinon CE 3 Memotron	1978	45-55
Chinon CE 4	1979	25-40
Chinon CE 4s	1981	25-40
Chinon CE 5	1983	45-55
Chinon CE II Memotron	1976	55-65
Chinon CE Memotron	1974	55-65
Chinon CE-4 Memotron	1979	55-65
Chinon CE-4s	1981	55-65
Chinon CE-5	1982	45-55
Chinon CG-5	1982	55-65
Chinon CM 3	1979	35-45
Chinon CM 4	1980	25-40
Chinon CM 5	1982	35-45
Chinon CM 7	1987	45-55
Chinon CM-3	1978	45-55
Chinon CM-4	----	20-40
Chinon CM-4s	1981	45-55
Chinon CM-5	----	25-45
Chinon CM-7	1987	55-65
Chinon CP 5	1983	45-55
Chinon CP 6	1985	45-55
Chinon CP 9 AF	1988	45-55

Manufacturer-model	Year	€
Chinon CP X	1985	55-65
Chinon CP-5	1984	75-85
Chinon CP-6	1985	75-85
Chinon CP-7	1986	55-65
Chinon CP-7M	----	20-30
Chinon CP-9 AF	1988	75-85
Chinon Cp-9 Af (nera)	----	55-65
Chinon CS	----	20-40
Chinon CX	1975	25-40
Chinon CXII	----	50-65
Chinon DP-5	----	20-30
Chinon DSL	----	20-30
Chinon Genesis	1988	45-55
Chinon Genesis II	1989	45-55
Chinon Genesis III	1990	55-65
Chinon Genesis IV	1992	80-90
Chinon GL-AF	----	25-30
Chinon Handy	----	15-25
Chinon Infrafocus 35F-MA -	----	35-45
Chinon M1	1973	45-55
Chinon M95000	----	18-28
Chinon Monami AF	----	15-25
Chinon Splash AF	----	15-20
Chinonflex	1966	55-65

Cimko

Manufacturer-model	Year	€
Cimko LS-1	1976	30-50

Ciro

Manufacturer-model	Year	€
Ciro 35 Black (black)	----	250-300
Ciro 35 S	----	25-45
Ciro-Flex Alphax	----	25-40
Ciro-Flex Model E	----	80-100

Conley

Manufacturer-model	Year	€
Conley 5x7 Revolving	----	280-300
Conley Camera Co. Kewpie N. 3A	----	45-60
Conley Camera Co. Kewpie N. 3	----	20-40
Conley Camera Co. No. 2A	----	35-50
Camera Co. Citex-Snap-Shot	----	80-100
Conley No. 1 5X7	----	170-190

Contax

Manufacturer-model	Year	€
Contaflex	1935	1.400-1600
Contaflex I	1953	130-150
Contaflex II	1954	60-70
Contaflex III, IV	1957	160-180
Contaflex Super	1959	70-90
Contaflex Super BC	1967	190-210
Contarex (Ciclope)	1960	500-600
Contarex (Ciclope), black	1960	2000-2200
Contarex Hologon	1964	2500-2700
Contarex Professional	1967	1000-1200
Contarex SE, chrome	1970	1000-1200
Contarex SE, black	1970	1.000-1200
Contarex Special	1960	800-1000
Contarex Super	1968	400-550
Contarex Super B	1962	130-150
Contarex Super, black	1968	1400-1600
Contax 137 MA	1983	150-170
Contax 137 MD	1980	150-170
Contax 139 Quartz	1979	110-130
Contax 139 Quartz SLR	----	170-190
Contax 159 MM	1984	190-220
Contax 167 MT	1987	120-140

Manufacturer-model	Year	€
Contax 645	1999	1.100-1200
Contax 645 AF	1999	1400-1600
Contax Aria	1998	200-220
Contax AX	1996	450-500
Contax D	1953	150-170
Contax E	1955	120-140
Contax F	1957	90-110
Contax FB	1956	90-110
Contax FM	1957	100-120
Contax G1	1994	200-240
Contax G2	1996	350-380
Contax I a	1932	1200-1400
Contax I b	1933	600-750
Contax I c	1934	550-650
Contax I d	1935	750-800
Contax I e	1935	750-780
Contax I f	1935	550-580
Contax II	1936	550-650
Contax II	1945	3500-3700
Contax II a	1954	240-270
Contax III	1936	220-250
Contax III a	1951	240-260
Contax N1	2000	300-320
Contax NX	2002	200-220

Manufacturer-model	Year	€
Contax RTS	1975	150-170
Contax RTS II	1982	130-150
Contax RTS II Quartz	1982	190-220
Contax RTS III	1990	600-700
Contax RTS gold	1981	1200-1400
Contax RX	1995	290-310
Contax S	1949	280-300
Contax S 2	1992	400-450
Contax S2b	----	400-500
Contax ST	1992	400-450
Contax T Silver (silver)	----	300-320
Contax T2	1990	200-220
Contax T2 nera	1990	400-450
Contax T2 oro	1990	250-280
Contax T2 oro	1990	400-420
Contax T3	----	1000-1200
Contax T3D	----	1250-1500
Contax TVS	----	150-180
Contax TVS II	----	180-200
Contax TVS III	----	300-350

Contessa-Nettel

Manufacturer-model	Year	€
Contessa-Nettel	----	55-70

Cosina

Manufacturer-model	Year	€
Cosina 4000S	1976	40-60
Cosina C1/C1s	1992	40-60
Cosina C2	1993	40-60
Cosina CS-1	1979	70-90
Cosina CS-2	1979	70-90
Cosina CS-3	1979	80-100
Cosina CSL	1978	50-70
Cosina CT 1	1980	30-50
Cosina CT 1 Super	1983	40-60
Cosina CT 10	1979	50-70
Cosina CT 1A	1980	40-60
Cosina CT 2	1979	40-60
Cosina CT 20	1980	40-60
Cosina CT 3	1980	40-60
Cosina CT 4	1979	40-60
Cosina CT 7	1980	40-60
Cosina CT 9	1986	40-60
Cosina CT 90F	1988	40-60
Cosina CT-1 G	1983	40-60
Cosina CT-1 Super	1983	40-60
Cosina E1 Solar	1994	40-60
Cosina Hi Lite	1971	40-60

Manufacturer-model	Year	€
Cosina Hi Lite 405	1976	40-60
Cosina Hi-Lite DLR	1975	40-60
Cosina Hi-Lite EC	1973	40-60
Cosina Hi-Lite ECS	1975	40-60
Cosina 107-SW	----	140-180
Cosina 1000S	----	45-65
Cosina PM-1	----	30-50
Cosina / Argus STL 1000	----	30-50

Crystar

Manufacturer-model	Year	€
Crystar Sunscope	----	85-100
Crystar Sunscope 35	----	100-120

Dacora

Manufacturer-model	Year	€
Dacora	1940-1945	290-310
Dacora Dignette	1955	40-60

Demaria

Manufacturer-model	Year	€
Demaria Monte-Carlo	----	60-80

Ducati

Manufacturer-model	Year	€
Ducati Sogno I	1938	1100-1400
Ducati Sogno II	1950	340-380
Ducati Simplex 18x24		800-1000

Duflex

Manufacturer-model	Year	€
Duflex	1949	4000

Durst

Manufacturer-model	Year	€
Durst 66	1966	90-110

Ears

Manufacturer-model	Year	€
Ears Ksx Black	----	45-60

Edixa

Manufacturer-model	Year	€
Edixa 135 AF	----	30-45
Edixa C 3000	----	140-160
Edixa Electronic	1962	110-130
Edixa Electronic	1970	290-310
Edixa II-L	----	60-80
Edixa Mat B	1958	100-120
Edixa Mat C	1958	120-140
Edixa Mat D	1961	130-150
Edixa Mat Reflex	1970	90-110
Edixa Prismaflex LTL	1968	110-130
Edixa Prismat LTL	1969	100-120
Edixa Reflex	1954	90-110
Edixa Reflex A	1956	100-120
Edixa Reflex B	1957	100-120
Edixa T1000	1976	40-60
Edixa T500	1976	40-60

Effebi

Manufacturer-model	Year	€
Effebi	1950	2000-2400

Ensign

Manufacturer-model	Year	€
Ensign 2 1/4B	----	100-120
Ensign 220	1950	50-70
Ensign All Distance	----	20-40
Ensign E29	1929	80-100
Ensign E29	1930	20-40
Ensign Pocket Twenty 2	----	20-40
Ensign Selfix 16-20	1950	35-45
Ensign Selfix 320	----	55-75

Ernamann

Manufacturer-model	Year	€
Ernemann Ernoflex Model I	----	420-440
Ernemann Rolf I	----	40-65

Exakta

Manufacturer-model	Year	€
Exa	1951	120-140
Exa 500	1967	50-70
Exa I	1962	70-90
Exa I A	1964	40-60
Exa I B	1977	80-100
Exa II	1962	220-240
Exakta 42 Twin	----	25-45
Exakta 66	----	700-900
Exakta EDX 2	1977	40-60
Exakta EDX 3	1978	50-70
Exakta Exa 1a	1965	40-60
Exakta FE 2000	1977	40-60
Exakta HS 10	1983	40-60
Exakta HS 40	1988	40-60
Exakta I Kine	1936	1280-1450
Exakta Ihagee (chrome)	----	75-95
Exakta II	1949	220-240
Exakta Kine Exakta 1	1936	130-155
Exakta Kine Exakta II	1949	150-175
Exakta Real	1966	1200-1400
Exakta Real, black	1966	3000-3500
Exakta RTL 1000	1970	90-120
Exakta RTL1000	----	55-80

Manufacturer-model	Year	€
Exakta TL 1000	1976	40-60
Exakta TL 500	1976	40-60
Exakta Twin TL	1973	80-100
Exakta Varex	1950	150-175
Exakta Varex II a	1957	190-220
Exakta Varex II b	1957	100-120
Exakta VP model B	----	340-380
Exakta VX 1000	1967	130-160
Exakta VX 1000 (Varex)	1967	30-45
Exakta VX 500	1969	40-60
Exakta VX 500 (Varex)	1969	40-60

Fed

Manufacturer-model	Year	€
Fed 1	1934	600-650
Fed 1	1946	90-120
Fed 2, series	1955	70-90
Fed 2, Type D F150	----	85-100
Fed 3, series	1961	40-60
Fed 4, series	1964	30-50
Fed 5, black	----	85-100
Fed 5, series	1977	30-50

Ferrania

Manufacturer-model	Year	€
Ferrania 3M 3025	----	45-60
Ferrania 3M Eura	----	60-80
Ferrania Alfa	----	75-90
Ferrania Condor I	----	160-180
Ferrania Condoretta	1946-1952	60-90
Ferrania Elioflex	1958	100-120
Ferrania Eta	1949	60-80
Ferrania Euralux 34	----	60-85
Ferrania Euramatica	1964	28-40
Ferrania Eurarapid	----	40-60
Ferrania Galileo	----	60-80
Ferrania Ibis	1955	60-80
Ferrania Ibis 34	----	35-45
Ferrania Ibis 44	----	34-50
Ferrania Lince	----	60-75
Ferrania Lince 3	----	70-85
Ferrania Lince 3S	----	90-110
Ferrania Rondine	1948	40-60
Ferrania Solaris	----	40-60
Ferrania Veramatic	1964	28-40

Fiumea

Manufacturer-model	Year	€
Fiumea	1950	1300-1500

Foca

Manufacturer-model	Year	€
Foca	1946	130-150
Foca PF 2	1946	120-140
Foca PF 2B	1947	110-130
Foca PF 3	1951	140-160
Foca PF 3L	1958	200-220
Foca Standard	1953	120-140
Foca Universal	1948	180-200
Focarex Automatic	1960	190-210
Focarex I	1959	200-240
Focarex II	1962	350-400
Focasport Compact	----	30-50

Folmer & Schwing

Manufacturer-model	Year	€
Folmer & Schwing Kodak	----	250-280

Franka

Manufacturer-model	Year	€
Franka AF-300	1980	20-35
Franka MX-I		30-50
Franka Solida 1	1954	110-130
Franka Super Frankarette	----	60-70

Fuji

Manufacturer-model	Year	€
Fuijca STX-1 Chrome	----	85-100
Fuji AX Multi Program	1985	50-70
Fuji Cardia Mini	----	35-50
Fuji DL-200	----	40-60
Fuji Fotorama FP-1 Prof.	----	450-550
Fuji Fujica 35 Auto-M	----	60-75
Fuji Fujica 35-Se	----	60-80
Fuji Fujica Ax-3 Black	----	65-85
Fuji Fujica Half	----	60-85
Fuji Fujica St701 Chrome	----	105-120
Fuji Fujicaflex TLR	----	1000-1400
Fuji HD-M	----	25-45
Fuji Instax Mini 10	----	25-40

Manufacturer-model	Year	€
Fuji Instax Mini 20	----	20-40
Fuji Instax Mini 25	----	45-60
Fuji Instax Mini 50S	----	40-60
Fuji Instax Mini 8	----	45-65
Fuji STX 2	1984	50-75
Fuji TW-3	----	45-60
Fuji Work Record	----	25-40
Fujica 250	----	25-40
Fujica AX 1	1982	50-80
Fujica AX 3	1980	60-85
Fujica AX 5	1980	60-90
Fujica AX MP	1985	50-75
Fujica AZ 1	1977	70-95
Fujica Fuji 350	----	25-50
Fujica G 617	1984	1200-1400
Fujica GA 645 i Prof.	1998	900-1200
Fujica GA 645 Zi	1998	500-600
Fujica GS 645	1995	290-320
Fujica GS 645 S	1984	280-320
Fujica GS 645 W	1983	350-385
Fujica GSW 670 III Prof.	1999	750-795
Fujica GSW 690	1984	450-480
Fujica GW 690 II	1986	650-700
Fujica GW 690 III Prof.	1992	850-900
Fujica GX 617	1994	2000-2400
Fujica GX 680	1989	300-350

Manufacturer-model	Year	€
Fujica GX 680 II Prof.	1994	450-500
Fujica GX 680 III	1999	600-700
Fujica ST 601	1976	40-60
Fujica ST 605	1977	50-70
Fujica ST 605 N	1979	50-70
Fujica ST 701	1971	50-75
Fujica ST 705	1977	60-85
Fujica ST 705 W	1979	50-70
Fujica ST 801	1973	100-125
Fujica ST 901	1974	70-95
Fujica ST 901 A.E.	1974	110-135
Fujica ST-F	1979	20-40
Fujica STX-1	1980	40-60
Fujica STX1 N	1982	50-75
Fujica STX-2	1985	40-60
Fujifilm Instax "Hello Kitty"	----	75-100
Fujifilm instax mini 25	----	20-35
Fujifilm instax mini 50S	----	45-60
Fujifilm Instax Mini 70	----	55-70
Fujifilm Instax MINI 7s	----	30-45
Fujifilm Instax Mini 90	----	85-110
Fujifilm Klasse	----	250-300
Fujifilm Klasse W	----	450-550
Fujifilm Quicksnap	----	20-40

Gabrj

Manufacturer-model	Year	€
Gabrj icaf	1937	200-220

Gamma

Manufacturer-model	Year	€
Gamma I	1947	1000-1400
Gamma III	1950	1400-1600
Gamma Roma	----	180-200

Gomz

Manufacturer-model	Year	€
FK 13 13X18	----	200-250
Gomz Lubitel 2	----	80-100
Smena	----	40-50
Smena 1	----	40-50
Smena 2	----	40-50
Gomz Tourist 6x9	----	140-180

Graflex

Manufacturer-model	Yea	€
Crown Graphic	----	45-60
Graflex 3-1/4 X 4-1/4 Pre-	----	220-240
Graflex 4X5 Speed Graphic	----	100-140
Graflex Anniversary Speed	----	550-600
Graflex Baby Speed Graphic	----	130-160
Graflex Century 35	----	90-110
Graflex Century 35a	----	75-95
Graflex Crown Graphic 4x5"	----	170-190
Graflex Graphic 35	----	65-80
Graflex Graphic View II 4x5	----	120-140
Graflex Miniature Speed Graphic	----	170-210
Graflex R. B. Series D	----	300-400
Graflex Series B 3¼ x 4¼	----	280-320
Graflex Speed Graphic 34	----	240-285
Graflex Type K-20 Aircraft Camera	----	700-900
Graflex Xl	----	700-900
Graflex XL Medium Format SLR	----	350-450

Gundlach

Manufacturer-model	Year	€
Gundlach Korona No. 30	----	140-160
Korona 5x7	----	200-250
Korona III	----	70-90

Haking

Manufacturer-model	Year	€
Haking CFML	----	20-30
Haking Halina 35X	----	20-40
Haking HG-1	1985	30-45
Haking HG-2	1985	30-45
Haking Vision	----	20-40
Haking Vision 1800 TL	----	20-40
Haking Vision III	----	25-35

Hanimex

Manufacturer-model	Year	€
Hanimex 110	----	20-40
Hanimex 110 DF	----	28-45
Hanimex 110 TF	----	20-40
Hanimex 35 EE	----	40-60
Hanimex 35 HL	----	25-50
Hanimex 35 Micro		18-30
Hanimex 35R	1976	30-40
Hanimex 35RS	----	25-40
Hanimex 35SE	----	20-40

Manufacturer-model	Year	€
Hanimex 35SL	----	25-40
Hanimex anfibia	----	28-45
Hanimex C550	----	25-40
Hanimex compact A	----	28-40
Hanimex Flash Reflex	1980	30-50
Hanimex IC 200	----	20-40
Hanimex IC 3000	----	20-40
Hanimex Loadmatic C550	----	20-35
Hanimex Pocket Camera 100	----	18-30
Hanimex Pocket Camera 108F	----	18-30
Hanimex Praktica 66-	----	80-100
Hanimex Praktica LTL	----	30-50
Hanimex Praktica Nova 1b	----	75-90
Hanimex Praktica Nova IB	----	25-45
Hanimex Praktica Super TL	----	80-95
Hanimex Praktica super TL	1969	90-110
Hanimex Snapshot Brite	----	28-45
Hanimex Snapshot metal	----	28-45
Hanimex Tele 110	----	20-40
Hanimex VC3200	----	20-35
Hanimex VEF	----	20-40
Super TL SLR	----	50-65

Hasselblad

Manufacturer-model	Year	€
Hasselblad 1000 F	1952	250-270
Hasselblad 1600 F	1948	450-470
Hasselblad 2000 FC	1977	1900-2200
Hasselblad 2000 FC/M	1981	200-250
Hasselblad 2000 FC/M oro	1985	1200-1450
Hasselblad 2003 FCW	1988	600-750
Hasselblad 201 F	1995	400-500
Hasselblad 202 FA	1998	900-1100
Hasselblad 202FA	----	1450-1750
Hasselblad 203 FE	1996	1300-1500
Hasselblad 205 FCC	1997	4000-4400
Hasselblad 205TCC	----	1850-2200
Hasselblad 500 C	1957	500-650
Hasselblad 500 C/M	1970	300-350
Hasselblad 500 Classic	1989	1200-1400
Hasselblad 500 EL	1965	200-250
Hasselblad 500 EL/M	1970	250-280
Hasselblad 500 ELX	1984	250-300
Hasselblad 501 C	1995	450-550
Hasselblad 501 C/M	1997	800-900
Hasselblad 503 CW	1996	450-550
Hasselblad 503 CX	1988	300-400
Hasselblad 503CXi	----	900-1200

Manufacturer-model	Year	€
Hasselblad 553 ELX	1988	400-550
Hasselblad 555 ELD	----	750-950
Hasselblad 555 ELD	1998	750-900
Hasselblad 903 SWC	1988	2200-2400
Hasselblad 903SWC	----	2400-3000
Hasselblad 905 SWC	2000	2500-2750
Hasselblad 905SWC	----	5500-7500
Hasselblad H1	----	1800-2000
Hasselblad H1	2002	1800-1950
Hasselblad H2	----	1550-2000
Hasselblad SWA	1954	1300-1500
Hasselblad SWC	1959	1700-1900
Hasselblad SWC/M	1979	2000-2400
Hasselblad Xpan	1998	1000-1400
Hasselblad Xpan II	2003	1300-1500

Herold

Manufacturer-model	Year	€
Herold Acro-flash	----	32-45
Herold Photo Master	----	28-40
Herold Sparta fold	----	70-90
Herold Spartus 120	1953*	40-60
Herold Spartus 35	----	70-90
Herold Spartus 35 F	----	35-45

Honeywell

Manufacturer-model	Year	€
Honeywell Electric Eye 35	----	80-120
Honeywell Electric Eye 35r	----	29-40
Honeywell Pentax ES II	----	70-90
Honeywell Pentax H1 a SLR	----	65-90
Honeywell Pentax H3 SLR	----	40-60
Honeywell Pentax HV3	----	30-50
Honeywell Pentax Sp 1000	----	70-90

Horizon

Manufacturer-model	Year	€
Horizon	1967	180-220
Horizon HZ 35	----	20-45
Horizon Kompakt	----	100-130
Horizon 202	1995	220-250

Houghton

Manufacturer-model	Year	€
Houghton-Butcher	1923	70-90
Houghton Butcher Ensign E29	1930*	60-85
Houghton Butcher Ensign Junior	----	70-90
Houghton Ensign Popular Reflex	----	100-130
Houghton Ensign Special Reflex	----	128-150
Houghton Ensignette 2	----	90-120

Ica

Manufacturer-model	Year	€
Ica Icarette	----	45-60
Ica Jearette 503	----	140-160
Icarex 35 BM	1969	130-150
Icarex 35 S BM	1969	150-170
Icarex 35 S TM	1969	240-260
Icarex 35 TM	1969	130-150

Ihagee

Manufacturer-model	Year	€
Ihagee Parvola	----	150-170
Ihagee Pionier	----	70-90

Ilford

Manufacturer-model	Year	€
Ilford Limited Advocate	----	50-70
Ilford SM	----	40-60
Ilford Sporti	----	22-45
Ilford Sportina Rapid	----	20-40
Ilford Sportsman	----	22-45
Ilford Witness	1951	3000-3500

Iloca

Manufacturer-model	Year	€
Iloca I a	----	65-80
Iloca II	----	80-100
Iloca II a	----	40-60
Iso Bilux	1950	1700-1850
Iloca Quick	----	50-70
Iloca Rapid A1	----	40-60
Iloca Rapid II	----	28-45

Iso

Manufacturer-model	Year	€
Iso Reporter	1953	1300-1500
Iso Standard	1953	1300-1500

Janua

Manufacturer-model	Year	€
Janua	1948	2500-2750
Janua San Giorgio Essegi	----	2200-2400

Kalimar

Manufacturer-model	Year	€
Kalimar 35-55	----	15-28
Kalimar 3d	----	55
Kalimar Autowind	----	20
Kalimar AW Auto Weather	----	15
Kalimar AW-10	----	15-28
Kalimar C-64	----	55
Kalimar DK-3	----	28
Kalimar FF-10	----	20
Kalimar FF-10	----	20-40
Kalimar K-90	----	30
Kalimar KX-7000	----	25-50
Kalimar LX:11	----	28
Kalimar Spirit	----	25-40
Kalimar SR 200	----	40
Kalimar SR200	----	25-45

Kershaw

Manufacturer-model	Year	€
Kershaw 110	----	40-60
Kershaw 630	1954-	45-65
King Penguin Eight-20	1951	40-55

Kiev

Manufacturer-model	Year	€
Kiev	1948	1500-1700
Kiev 10	----	70-85
Kiev -15	----	45-55
Kiev 15 TEE	1974	110-130
Kiev 16C-3	----	45-55
Kiev 19	----	45-55
Kiev 19	1990	100-120
Kiev 2	1950	150-200
Kiev 2 II	----	50-65
Kiev 20	----	65-75
Kiev 2A	----	80-110
Kiev 3	----	70-85
Kiev 3 A	1956	45-60
Kiev 3 A	1956	40-55
Kiev 30	1982	20-30
Kiev 4	1964	40-50
Kiev 4A	----	40-55
Kiev 4M	----	45-60
Kiev 5	1967	80-100
Kiev 6	----	70-90
Kiev 6 C	1962	110-130
Kiev 60	1984	110-125
Kiev 80	1975	120-140

Manufacturer-model	Year	€
Kiev 88	1980	140-160
Kiev -88	----	100-120
Kiev 88 TTL	1980	190-210
Kiev Automat 10	1965	130-150
Kiev II, IIa	1948	70-90
Kiev III	1952	50-70
Kiev III, IV	1955	50-70
Kiev-17	----	40-55
Kiev-19M	----	40-55
Kiev-303	----	18-30
Kiev-60 TTL	----	70-90

Kochmann

Manufacturer-model	Year	€
Kochmann Reflex Korelle	----	250-270
Kochmann Reflex-Korelle Ia	----	150-170

Kodak

Manufacturer-model	Year	€
Kodak 110 Pocket Instamatic	----	28-35
Kodak 126 Instamatic 104	----	20-35
Kodak 126 Instamatic 55 X	----	20-35
Kodak 1-A Autographic Special	----	80-100
Kodak 2D	----	180-220
Kodak 35 Rangefinder	----	65-85
Kodak 4x5 Master View Camera	----	140-160
Kodak Analyst Technical Instant	----	40-55
Kodak Autographic Junior	----	40-60
Kodak Automatic 35	----	28-35
Kodak Automatic 35f	----	40-60
Kodak Baby Brownie Special	----	25-40
Kodak Bantam	----	45-60
Kodak Bantam RF	----	80-100
Kodak Bantam Special	----	280-350
Kodak Box Brownie 44	----	40-60
Kodak Box Brownie Hawkeye	----	60-80
Kodak Box Brownie Model 1	----	80-100
Kodak Box Brownie Portrait N. 2	----	50-70
Kodak Box Brownie Six 16	----	28-35
Kodak Box Brownie Six 20 Junior	----	50-780
Kodak Box Brownie Six 20 Mod.	----	50-70
Kodak Box Brownie Six 20 Mod.	----	80-100

Manufacturer-model	Year	€
Kodak Box Brownie Target Six 16	----	40-60
Kodak Box Brownie Target Six 20	----	40-60
Kodak Box Hawkeie Model C N. 2	----	80-100
Kodak Box Hawkeie Model C N.2	----	80-100
Kodak Brownie Starmait	----	45-60
Kodak Colorsnap 35	----	45-60
Kodak Duaflex II	----	15-25
Kodak Duo Six-20	----	55-70
Kodak Easishare	----	50-65
Kodak Ektagraphic Ef		60-75
Kodak Ektar	1949	350-400
Kodak Ektralite 10		40-60
Kodak Filmplate Premo Special	----	45-65
Kodak Flash Bantam	----	45-65
Kodak Folding Pocket 105	----	100-150
Kodak Funsaver 35	----	22-40
Kodak Funsaver Pocket Daylight	----	22-35
Kodak Hawk-Eye 2a Model B	1926	70-90
Kodak Hawkeye Instamatic R4	----	28-40
Kodak Instamatic 10 pocket	----	15-20
Kodak Instamatic 100	----	28-45
Kodak Instamatic 104	----	24-40
Kodak Instamatic 124	----	34-45
Kodak Instamatic 133	----	28-40
Kodak Instamatic 134	----	28-40
Kodak Instamatic 150	----	24-40

Manufacturer-model	Year	€
Kodak Instamatic 25	----	22-40
Kodak Instamatic 277X	----	15-20
Kodak Instamatic 300	----	22-40
Kodak Instamatic 304	----	24-40
Kodak Instamatic 314	----	20-40
Kodak Instamatic 404	----	22-40
Kodak Instamatic 414	----	28-40
Kodak Instamatic 500	----	40-60
Kodak Instamatic 700	----	40-60
Kodak Instamatic 77x	----	28-40
Kodak Instamatic 800	----	40-60
Kodak Instamatic Camera 66x	----	28-40
Kodak Instamatic X15	----	10-25
Kodak Jiffy Six-16	----	25-40
Kodak Junior 620	----	100-120
Kodak KV270	----	25-40
Kodak Medalist I	----	170-220
Kodak Monitor Six-20	----	25-40
Kodak Motormatic 35	----	58-75
Kodak Motormatic 35f	----	58-70
Kodak N. 1 Pocket	----	20-40
Kodak N. 1 Pocket Kodak Junior	----	85-100
Kodak N. 1a Folding Pocket	----	50-70
Kodak N. 1a Special Model Aa	----	90-110
Kodak N. 2 Folding Pocket	----	95-120
Kodak N. 3 Folding Brownie	----	140-160

Manufacturer-model	Year	€
Kodak N. 4 Folding Model B	----	325-370
Kodak No. 10 Cirkut	----	2800-
Kodak Pocket N. 1	----	28-40
Kodak Pony 135 Model B	----	45-60
Kodak Pony 828	----	60-80
Kodak Pony II	----	32-45
Kodak Proemette	----	100-120
Kodak Recomar Model 33	----	40-60
Kodak Retina Automatic III	----	28-40
Kodak Retina I a	----	29-40
Kodak Retina I b	----	80-100
Kodak Retina I Type 010	----	70-90
Kodak Retina II c Type 020	----	70-90
Kodak Retina II f	----	70-90
Kodak Retina II Type 142	----	90-110
Kodak Retina III c	----	70-90
Kodak Retina IIS	----	35-45
Kodak Retinette 1b	----	100-120
Kodak Retinette I a	----	40-60
Kodak Retinette IIB	----	40-60
Kodak Retinette Type 012	----	200-220
Kodak Retinette Type 017	----	72-90
Kodak S100 EF,	----	45-60
Kodak Signet 40	----	60-80
Kodak Signet 50	----	45-60

Manufacturer-model	Year	€
Kodak Signet 80	----	35-55
Kodak Six-16	----	25-40
Kodak Stretch 35	----	28-45
Kodak Tourist	----	28-45
Kodak Tourist 620	----	70-90
Kodak Vest Pocket	----	140-160
Kodak Vollenda 620	----	250-300
Kodak Weekend 35	----	28-45
Kodak Z 740	----	120-140
Replica per 100° Anniversario	1988	300-400

Konica

Manufacturer-model	Year	€
Konica 261	----	20-35
Konica A4	----	55-70
Konica A4 (silver)	----	45-60
Konica ACOM-1	----	40-60
Konica Aerial Type G	----	400-460
Konica Aiborg Super	----	40-60
Konica Auto S2	----	55-70
Konica Auto-Reflex	1965	120-140
Konica Autoreflex A	1969	60-80

Manufacturer-model	Year	€
Konica Autoreflex A3	----	25-40
Konica Autoreflex T	1968	120-140
Konica Autoreflex T3	1973	140-160
Konica Autoreflex T4	1978	60-80
Konica Autoreflex TC	1976	80-100
Konica Autorex P	1969	90-110
Konica Big mini BM-201	----	120-140
Konica Big Mini F	----	140-170
Konica Big mini Point & Shoot	----	25-35
Konica Bigmini A4	----	70-90
Konica BM-S630	----	20-40
Konica C35	----	25-40
Konica C35 V	----	45-60
Konica EE Matic Deluxe	----	20-35
Konica EFP 2	----	25-35
Konica F	1960	900-1000
Konica FC1	1980	50-75
Konica FF-88D	----	65-80
Konica FP1	1980	40-60
Konica FS	1960	30-55
Konica FS1	1979	60-80
Konica FT1	1983	70-90
Konica Genba Kantoku	----	25-40
Konica Hexar	1993	550-650
Konica Hexar silver	1997	200-250

Manufacturer-model	Year	€
Konica Hexar classica	1993	350-400
Konica Hexar oro	1993	900-1000
Konica Hexar RF	----	700-900
Konica Hexar Rhodium	----	600-750
Konica IIB-m	----	45-65
Konica Kanpai	----	50-70
Konica Lexio 70	----	70-85
Konica MG Auto	----	30-50
Konica Minolta Maxxum 50	----	25-40
Konica Minolta Zoom 130c	----	20-35
Konica Mt-9	----	25-40
Konica Pearl III	----	140-180
Konica Pearl IV	----	400-500
Konica Pop EF-80	----	25-40
Konica Rapid Omega	----	550-700
Konica Revio Z3 APS	----	20-40
Konica S3	----	45-60
Konica Standa Big Mini	----	75-95
Konica TCX	1984	50-70
Konica Wide 28	----	80-110

Kowa

Manufacturer-model	Year	€
Kowa 35N	----	25-40
Kowa E	1962	30-55
Kowa H	----	25-40
Kowa H	1963	30-55
Kowa SE	1963	70-90
Kowa SER	1969	30-60
Kowa SET	1967	30-60
Kowa Set R2	----	35-55
Kowa SETR	1970	30-55
Kowa Six	1968	200-250
Kowa Six MM	1972	260-320
Kowa Super 66	1974	290-340
Kowa UW190	1972	400-450
Kowaflex	1960	130-160

Kristall

Manufacturer-model	Year	€
Kristall 53	1953	2400-2700
Kristall II	1950	1400-1650
Kristall II S	1951	400-600
Kristall III S	1952	1300-1500
Kristall R	1954	900-1100

Kyocera

Manufacturer-model	Year	€
Kyocera Dental Eye III	----	250-300
Kyocera LYNX	----	25-40
Kyocera P. mini 2 Panorama	----	40-60
KYOCERA T Scope 2 AF	----	160-185
Kyocera T Zoom	----	250-280
Kyocera Yashica 230-AF	----	50-75
Kyocera Yashica Acclaim 100	----	30-50
Kyocera Yashica EZS Zoom	----	55-70
Kyocera Yashica T4	----	150-180
Kyocera Yashica Zoom 120	----	30-50
Kyocera Yashica Zoom 70	----	30-50
Kyocera Yashica Zoom 90	----	30-50
Kyocera Yashica Zoomate 110	----	45-65
Kyocera Yashica Zoomate 115	----	45-65
Kyocera Zoomate 165EF	----	120-160

Lamperti&Garbagnati

Manufacturer-model	Year	€
Lamperti & Garbagnati	1925	2950-3200

Leica

Manufacturer-model	Year	€
Leica II (D)	1932	300-350
Leica 0, reply	2000	1.800-2200
Leica 250 FF	1934	3.000-3400
Leica 250 GG	1935	4000-4500
Leica 72 Midland	1950	8000-10000*
Leica 72 Wetzlar	1950	10000-15000*
Leica CL	1973	400-450
Leica CL 50 Jahre	1975	900-1200
Leica Compur (B) Ring	1929	1600-1800
Leica Compur Dial	1926	4000-4500
Leica I (C)	1930	900-1200
Leica I (C)	1931	500-650
Leica I (A) Anastigmat	1925	30000-35000*
Leica I (A) Elmar	1926	700-900
Leica I (A) Elmax	1925	9000-11000*
Leica I (A) Hektor	1930	2800-3200
Leica I c	1949	380-420
Leica I f	1952	500-550
Leica I g	1957	2500-2700
Leica I Luxus	1929	20000-25000*
Leica I Luxus	1931	30000-35000*
Leica I Luxus reply	vari	1000-1200
Leica Ig Post	1957	900-1100

Manufacturer-model	Year	€
Leica II (D) nera	1932	450-550
Leica II c	1948	390-420
Leica II f	1951	500-550
Leica II f	1952	350-385
Leica II New York	1947	850-1000
Leica III	1939	1400-1600
Leica III (F)	1933	400-500
Leica III a (G)	1935	400-450
Leica III a (G), nera	1935	800-900
Leica III a, Montè en	1950	1500-1700
Leica III b	1938	1100-1300
Leica III c	1940	650-750
Leica III c K, cromata	1942	1800-2000
Leica III c K, grigia	1942	1250-1500
Leica III c, chrome	1940	1000-1200
Leica III c, gray	1940	2500-2700
Leica III d	1940	6000-6400*
Leica III f	1950	350-400
Leica III f	1952	500-550
Leica III f	1954	600-650
Leica III f Canada	1950	2800-3200
Leica III f Midland	1953	9000-11000*
Leica III f, black	1956	13000-15000*
Leica III g	1957	650-800
Leica III g Gold	1957	4000-4500

Manufacturer-model	Year	€
Leica III g, Canada	1957	950-1200
Leica III g, black	1960	5000-6000*
Leica III, black	1933	800-1000
Leica KE-7A	1980	4500-5000
Leica KS-15	1968	2000-2500
Leica Leicaflex, chrome	1964	250-300
Leica Leicaflex, black	1964	600-700
Leica M1	1959	750-850
Leica M1	1960	2600-2850
Leica M2 gray	1960	15000-17000*
Leica M2 I type	1957	450-600
Leica M2 I type, black	1958	2100-2300
Leica M2 II type, black	1958	2100-2300
Leica M2 III type	1958	900-1100
Leica M2, II type	1957	800-900
Leica M2-M	1966	2500-2700
Leica M3 I type	1954	1450-1650
Leica M3 I type Canada	1954	2000-2500
Leica M3 II type	1954	450-600
Leica M3 II type Canada	1954	1200-1400
Leica M3 III type	1957	2500-2700
Leica M3 III type Canada	1957	1500-1700
Leica M3 III type black	1957	6000-6500
Leica M3 III tupe gold	1957	40000-45000*
Leica M3 black	1959	3000-4000

Manufacturer-model	Year	€
Leica M3 Null series	1952	50000-56000*
Leica M4	1967	850-1000
Leica M4	1970	20000-25000*
Leica M4 50 Jahre	1975	2200-2600
Leica M4 Lacquerede	1967	4000-5000
Leica M4 Mot	1967	4000-5000
Leica M4 black	1967	1700-1950
Leica M4-2	1977	2400-2700
Leica M4-2 black	1977	650-900
Leica M4-2 gold	1979	2500-2700
Leica M4-P	1980	1200-1450
Leica M4-P	1983	750-900
Leica M4-P black	1980	900-1200
Leica M5	1971	900-1200
Leica M5 50 Jahre	1975	2000-2500
Leica M5 50 Jahre black	1975	1200-1500
Leica M5 black	1971	800-1000
Leica M6	1984	1500-1700
Leica M6 150 Jahre	1999	4500-5000
Leica M6 A. Bruckner	1996	4000-5000
Leica M6 Colombo	1992	4000-5000
Leica M6 Ein Stuck	1996	2100-2400
Leica M6 J Jubilee	1994	4000-4800
Leica M6 black	1998	1600-1950
Leica M6 Platinum	1989	5000-6000*

Manufacturer-model	Year	€
Leica M6 Titanium	1992	1000-1200
Leica M6 Traveler Set	1994	1700-1900
Leica M6 TTL	1998	1200-1450
Leica M6 TTL	2000	1500-1800
Leica M6TTL lacquerede	2000	3500-3850
Leica M6 TTL Millenium	2000	3000-3900
Leica M6 TTL Titanium	2001	1300-1450
Leica M6 William Klein	2001	ND
Leica M7 Hermès	2009	9500-11000*
Leica M7, series	2002	1400-1600
Leica M8 White edition	2009	5500-5800
Leica M8.2 safari	2009	7500-8500
Leica M9 Titanium	2010	21000-25000*
Leica M9-P Hermès	2012	27000-40000*
Leica MD	1964	450-600
Leica MD a	1966	450-600
Leica Md a Mot	1970	3000-3500
Leica MD-2	1980	400-600
Leica MP	1956	12000-14000*
Leica MP	2003	2200-2500
Leica MP Hermès	2003	9000-12000*
Leica MP, black	1956	14000-16000*
Leica MP2	1959	30000-35000*
Leica MP3 LHSA	2005	5000-6000*

Manufacturer-model	Year	€
Leica R 3	1976	250-300
Leica R 3 "Germany"	1976	900-1100
Leica R 3 mot	1978	200-300
Leica R 3 Safari	1976	500-600
Leica R 4	1980	250-300
Leica R 4 mot	1980	200-300
Leica R 4 S	1983	250-350
Leica R 4 S II	1986	350-400
Leica R 5	1987	350-400
Leica R 6	1988	600-700
Leica R 6.2	1993	700-800
Leica R 7	1992	400-500
Leica R 8	1996	650-750
Leica R 9	1900	850-950
Leica RE	1990	250-350
Leica SL	1968	300-400
Leica SL 2	1974	600-700
Leica SL 2 mot	1975	1000-1200
Leica SL mot	1978	500-600
Leica Standard (E)	1932	600-700
Leica Standard (E), nera	1932	600-700
Leica Standard New	1948	1900-2200
Leica Ur Reply	1975	350-500

Leidolf

Manufacturer-model	Year	€
Leidolf Leidox	----	100-120
Leidolf Lordomat	----	90-110
Leidolf Lordomatic II	----	40-55
Leidolf Lordox	----	40-55

Leotax

Manufacturer-model	Year	€
Leotax 6x4	----	150-170
Leotax F	----	200-220
Leotax G	1954	700-800
Leotax K	----	100-160
Leotax S	1952	200-220
Leotax Showa	----	140-160
Leotax Special A	1942	900-1150
Leotax Special B	1942	600-750
Leotax Special D II	1947	400-550
Leotax Special D III	1947	400-600
Leotax T, K, TV	1954	600-750

Linhof

Manufacturer-model	Year	€
Linhof 6x9 press	----	1000-1200
Linhof Kardan Color Monorail	----	4000-5000
Linhof Technika 4x5	----	1000-1400
Linhof Technika 70	----	400-600
Linhof Technikardan 45S 4x5	----	2000-2500
Linhof Technorama 612 PC II	1994	2000-2500
Linhof Technorama 617 S III	1996	2600-3000

Lomo (anche Smena)

Manufacturer-model	Year	€
Lomo Smena 1	----	35-50
Lomo Smena 2	----	35-50
Lomo Smena 3	----	29-40
Lomo Smena 4	----	45-60
Lomo Smena 5	----	75-80
Lomo Smena 6	----	45-55
Lomo Smena 7	----	29-40
Lomo Smena 8M	----	25-45
Lomo Smena 35	----	25-45
Lomo Smena M	----	70-85
Lomo Smena Rapid	----	29-40
Lomo Smena SL	----	45-60
Lomo Smena Stereo	----	85-95
Lomo Smena Symbol	----	35-45

Mamyia

Manufacturer-model	Year	€
Mamiya	1967	30-50
Mamiya	1975	60-80
Mamiya 1000/1000TL	1966	50-70
Mamiya 6	1986	560-320
Mamiya 7 II	1999	900-1100
Mamiya C22	----	220-240
Mamiya C220 f	1968	200-240
Mamiya C3	----	150-200
Mamiya C330 S	1969	250-300
Mamiya M645	1976	110-140
Mamiya M645 1000S	1977	250-300
Mamiya M645 AF	1999	1600-1800
Mamiya M645 E	1999	1100-1300
Mamiya M645 Junior	1980	200-250
Mamiya M645 Pro	1992	650-750
Mamiya M645 Pro TL	2000	800-900
Mamiya M645 Super	1986	370-420
Mamiya NC 1000	1977	80-110
Mamiya NC 1000S	1978	110-140
Mamiya Press Universal	1976	450-500
Mamiya RB 67	1970	350-400
Mamiya RB 67 Pro SD	1990	850-950
Mamiya RZ 67 Pro	1982	280-340

Manufacturer-model	Year	€
Mamiya RZ 67 Pro II	1993	500-550
Mamiya Sekor 1000 DTL	1966	30-45
Mamiya Sekor 1000 MSX	1976	50-60
Mamiya Sekor 2000 DTL	1971	60-70
Mamiya Sekor 500 DTL	1966	30-45
Mamiya Sekor 500 MSX	1976	40-55
Mamiya Sekor Auto XTL	1971	80-95
Mamiya Sekor DSX 1000	1974	30-45
Mamiya Sekor DTL 1000	1968	30-45
Mamiya Sekor MSX 1000	1976	40-55
Mamiya Super 23	1964	300-350
Mamiya ZE	1980	30-45
Mamiya ZE 2	1980	40-55
Mamiya ZE X	1981	80-95
Mamiya ZE2 Quartz	1980	40-55
Mamiya ZM	1982	60-75
Mamiya ZM Quartz	1982	50-65
Mamiyaflex C3	1962	130-145
Mamiyaflex C33	1965	180-200

Manhattan

Manufacturer-model	Yea	€
Optical Long Focus Cycle Wizard	-----	320-340
Optical Co. Wizard Cycle A 4x5	-----	350-400

Mansfield

Manufacturer-model	Year	€
Mansfield Eye-Tronic	----	65-75
Mansfield Skylark	----	82-95

Meikai

Manufacturer-model	Year	€
Meikai 4 Shooter	----	25-40
Meikai 4351R	----	20-40
Meikai AR-4400	----	25-40
Meikai EL X	----	65-90
Meikai TM AR-4367	----	20-40

Meopta

Manufacturer-model	Year	€
Meopta Flexaret IIA	1947	140-160
Meopta Flexaret IIIa	----	95-110
Meopta Flexaret IV	1950	160-180

Minolta

Manufacturer-model	Year	€
Minolta XE 5	1976	60-80
Minolta 35 B	1947	450-550
Minolta 35 II	1953	400-500
Minolta 35 IIB	1957	250-300
Minolta 35 Original	1947	1000-1200
Minolta 5000	1986	90-110
Minolta 7000	1985	110-130
Minolta 9000	1985	130-150
Minolta Autopak 550	----	60-80
Minolta Dynax 2 xi	1992	100-120
Minolta Dynax 3 xi	1991	100-120
Minolta Dynax 300 si	1994	100-120
Minolta Dynax 3000 i	1988	70-90
Minolta Dynax 303 si	1999	100-120
Minolta Dynax 3L	2003	45-65
Minolta Dynax 3xi	1991	45-65
Minolta Dynax 4	2000	45-65
Minolta Dynax 40	2004	40-55
Minolta Dynax 404 si	1999	100-125
Minolta Dynax 5 xi	1992	150-175
Minolta Dynax 500 si	1994	120-140
Minolta Dynax 500 si Clas	1997	130-150
Minolta Dynax 5000 i	1989	70-85

Manufacturer-model	Year	€
Minolta Dynax 500si Super	1995	45-65
Minolta Dynax 505 si	1998	120-140
Minolta Dynax 505 si Super	1998	30-45
Minolta Dynax 5xi	1992	40-60
Minolta Dynax 60	2004	40-60
Minolta Dynax 600 si	1995	100-120
Minolta Dynax 600 si Classic	1995	110-135
Minolta Dynax 7	1900	250-270
Minolta Dynax 7	2000	60-80
Minolta Dynax 7 xi	1991	100-120
Minolta Dynax 700 si	1993	120-140
Minolta Dynax 7000i	1988	80-100
Minolta Dynax 7xi	1991	45-65
Minolta Dynax 800 si	1997	150-170
Minolta Dynax 8000i	1990	90-110
Minolta Dynax 9	1999	400-450
Minolta Dynax 9 xi	1992	250-285
Minolta Dynax SP xi	1991	70-90
Minolta Dynax X-300s	1990	40-55
Minolta Dynax X-370s	1994	40-60
Minolta ER	1963	20-35
Minolta SR-1	1959	110-130
Minolta SR-1S	1964	40-60
Minolta SR-2	1958	400-450
Minolta SR-3	1960	45-65

Manufacturer-model	Year	€
Minolta SR-7	1962	80-100
Minolta SR-M	1970	650-750
Minolta SRT 100	1971	70-90
Minolta SRT 100	1971	45-65
Minolta SRT 100 B	1976	60-80
Minolta SRT 100 X	1977	80-100
Minolta SRT 100b	1976	60-80
Minolta SRT 100X	1977	60-75
Minolta SRT 101	1966	90-110
Minolta SRT 101	1966	80-95
Minolta SRT 101 B	1977	80-100
Minolta SRT 101b	1976	60-80
Minolta SRT 303	1976	100-120
Minolta SRT 303b	1976	60-80
Minolta SRT-303	1974	60-75
Minolta Vectis 100 BF	----	20-40
Minolta Vectis S-1 (Aps)	1996	150-170
Minolta Vectis S-100 (Aps)	1997	80-100
Minolta X 300	1984	70-90
Minolta X 300-S	1990	70-85
Minolta X 370-S	1994	70-85
Minolta X 500	1983	110-130
Minolta X 700	1982	100-120
Minolta XD 5	1979	100-130
Minolta XD 7	1977	100-120

Manufacturer-model	Year	€
Minolta XD-7	1978	120-140
Minolta XE	1974	70-90
Minolta XE 1	1975	80-100
Minolta XE 5	1976	90-110
Minolta XE 7	1975	110-130
Minolta XE-1	1976	90-110
Minolta XE-1 nera	1976	140-155
Minolta XG 1	1979	90-115
Minolta XG 2	1978	80-100
Minolta XG 9	1980	80-95
Minolta XG M	1981	70-85
Minolta XG S	1979	90-110
Minolta XG-1	1979	40-60
Minolta XG-2	1978	60-75
Minolta XG-9	1980	45-65
Minolta XG-M	1981	40-55
Minolta XG-S	1979	45-65
Minolta XM	1973	350-385
Minolta XM Motor	1976	600-650

Minox

Manufacturer-model	Year	€
Minox 110 S	----	120-140
Minox 35 AL	----	120-140
Minox 35 GL	----	80-95
Minox 35 GT	1981	220-240
Minox 35 ML	----	140-160
Minox 35 PE	----	80-100
Minox A Chrome	----	150-180
Minox A Chrome Wetzlar	----	200-250
Minox B Chrome	----	100-120
Minox B SPY	----	70-95
Minox BL Chrome	----	150-180
Minox C Chrome	----	100-120
Minox C Chrome FI (Italia)	----	150-180
Minox C nera	----	280-320
Minox CD 128 DB	----	40-55
Minox CD70	----	25-45
Minox EC	----	100-120
Minox EL	----	30-50
Minox III submini	----	150-180
Minox LX Platin	----	1300-1500
Minox Vef Riga Spy	----	800-1000

Miranda

Manufacturer-model	Year	€
Miranda Auto Sensorex EE	1972	50-70
Miranda Auto Sensorex EE2	1975	50-65
Miranda Automex I, II, III	1959	50-65
Miranda D	1960	50-70
Miranda DX 3	1975	40-60
Miranda dx-3	1975	70-85
Miranda F	1967	240-260
Miranda Fv	1968	90-110
Miranda FvT	1968	60-80
Miranda G	1965	60-85
Miranda GT	1966	100-125
Miranda RE II	1975	50-65
Miranda Sensomat	1969	70-85
Miranda Sensomat RE	1970	50-65
Miranda Sensomat RE II	1975	60-75
Miranda Sensorex	1967	40-55
Miranda Sensorex	1968	40-60
Miranda Sensorex II	1972	50-70
Miranda T	1956	400-450
Miranda T (Orion camera)	1953	1500-1800
Miranda TM	1976	80-100

Montranus

Manufacturer-model	Yea	€
Montanus Montiflex (Delmonta)	----	140-160
Montanus Plascaflex 6X6	----	300-340
Montanus Rocca	----	28-50
Montanus Solingen Ultraflex	----	700-900

Neoca

Manufacturer-model	Year	€
Neoca 2S	----	85-100
Neoca SV	----	580-620

Nicca

Manufacturer-model	Year	€
Nicca 3 S	1954	340-370
Nicca 33	1959	280-330
Nicca 4	1953	390-420
Nicca 5	1955	640-700
Nicca 5 L	1957	370-410
Nicca III L	1958	300-350
Nicca III, IIIA	1951	480-540
Nicca IIIB	1951	290-340
Nicca Nippon	1947	3000-3500
Nicca Nippon Original	1942	1100-1400
Nicca Nippon Standard	1948	2600-3000

Nikon

Manufacturer-model	Year	€
Nikon F	1963	600-750
Nikon F, nera	1963	600-800
Nikon 28Ti	----	250-300
Nikon 35Ti	----	200-250
Nikon Calypso Nikkor	1963	320-360
Nikon Calypso Nikkor II	1968	280-320
Nikon EL 2	1977	200-250
Nikon EL2	1977	290-340
Nikon EM	1979	80-120
Nikon F	1959	700-900
Nikon F	1960	300-450
Nikon F 100	1999	250-300
Nikon F 301	1985	90-120
Nikon F 401	1987	90-120
Nikon F 401 S	1989	90-120
Nikon F 401 X	1991	90-120
Nikon F 50	1994	60-80
Nikon F 501	1986	60-80
Nikon F 60	1998	70-90
Nikon F 601 AF	1990	80-100
Nikon F 601 M	1990	60-85
Nikon F 65	2000	80-100
Nikon F 70	1994	70-95

Manufacturer-model	Year	€
Nikon F 80	2000	100-130
Nikon F 801	1988	80-95
Nikon F 801 S	1991	80-100
Nikon F 90	1992	100-125
Nikon F 90 S	2001	100-130
Nikon F 90 X	1994	120-145
Nikon F High Speed	1974	10000-12000*
Nikon F High Speed Sapporo	1972	10000-12000*
Nikon F KS-80A	1963	3000-3500
Nikon F black	1959	2500-3000
Nikon F black	1960	500-650
Nikon F Photomic	1962	200-250
Nikon F Photomic	1962	400-500
Nikon F Photomic FTn	1967	300-380
Nikon F Photomic FTn NASA	1968	2600-3200
Nikon F Photomic FTn, nera	1967	450-600
Nikon F Photomic T	1965	240-320
Nikon F Photomic TN	1966	250-350
Nikon F, motore 250, black	1960	1000-1400
Nikon F100	1999	230-280
Nikon F2	1971	290-340
Nikon F2-exposure meter DP1	1971	220-260
Nikon F2 (prismatico)	1971	300-350
Nikon F2 A-exposure meter	1977	300-340
Nikon F2 AS(expos. DP12)	1978	400-440

Manufacturer-model	Year	€
Nikon F2 H, high speed 1	1978	3200-3600
Nikon F2 Photomic	1971	210-250
Nikon F2 Photomic, black	1971	270-320
Nikon F2 S-exposure met. DP2	1973	250-300
Nikon F2 SB (exposure DP3)	1976	270-330
Nikon F2 SB Photomic	1976	400-500
Nikon F2 T	1979	1400-1600
Nikon F2 Titan	1976	1400-1550
Nikon F2, black	1971	400-500
Nikon F2A 25 Anniversary	1978	800-900
Nikon F2A Photomic	1977	290-320
Nikon F2AS Photomic	1977	450-500
Nikon F2H, high speed 2	1979	2900-3400
Nikon F2S Photomic	1973	330-400
Nikon F2S Photomic, nera	1973	340-400
Nikon F3	1980	300-370
Nikon F3 AF	1983	600-670
Nikon F3 HP	1983	250-300
Nikon F3 P	1983	450-500
Nikon F3 T	1982	550-600
Nikon F301	1985	90-120
Nikon F3HP	1983	400-500
Nikon F3P	1983	490-550
Nikon F3T	1983	500-600
Nikon F3T Champagne	1983	700-800

Manufacturer-model	Year	€
Nikon F4	1988	200-250
Nikon F4-exposure met. MB-20	1988	240-300
Nikon F4 E	1991	390-420
Nikon F4 S- expos. MB-21	1988	300-350
Nikon F401	1987	50-85
Nikon F401s	1989	60-95
Nikon F401X	1991	110-140
Nikon F4s	1988	290-330
Nikon F5	1996	550-600
Nikon F5 50 Anniversary	1998	900-1100
Nikon F-50	1994	100-140
Nikon F501	1986	90-120
Nikon F55	2002	110-140
Nikon F6	2001	800-900
Nikon F6	2004	1000-1250
Nikon F60	1998	80-100
Nikon F601 AF	1990	130-160
Nikon F601 M	1990	150-185
Nikon F65	2000	50-70
Nikon F-70	1994	120-145
Nikon F75	2003	40-65
Nikon F80	2000	110-125
Nikon F801	1988	70-90
Nikon F801s	1991	100-125
Nikon F-90	1992	110-140

Manufacturer-model	Year	€
Nikon F-90X	1994	120-150
Nikon FA	1983	200-250
Nikon FA gold	1984	1000-1250
Nikon FE	1978	120-145
Nikon FE 10	1997	80-100
Nikon FE 2	1983	150-200
Nikon FE2, black	1983	150-190
Nikon FG	1982	80-110
Nikon FG 20	1984	60-90
Nikon FM	1977	120-145
Nikon FM 2	1983	150-180
Nikon FM 2 New	1984	200-250
Nikon FM 2 Titan	1993	500-600
Nikon FM 3a	2001	400-500
Nikon FM-10	1997	80-100
Nikon FM2	1982	190-240
Nikon FM2, police	1982	2000-2500
Nikon FM2n	1984	140-170
Nikon FM2n, black	1984	350-400
Nikon I	1948	10000-
Nikon M	1949	3800-4300
Nikon M	1950	1800-2100
Nikon Nijkkormat EL	1972	120-160
Nikon Nijkkormat EL, black	1972	130-175
Nikon Nikkorex 35	1962	70-95

Manufacturer-model	Year	€
Nikon Nikkorex Auto 35	1964	100-125
Nikon Nikkorex F	1963	190-220
Nikon Nikkorex F, black	1963	900-1000
Nikon Nikkorex zoom	1963	170-220
Nikon Nikkorex Zoom 35	1963	100-140
Nikon Nikkormat EL	1972	140-180
Nikon Nikkormat EL-W	1976	170-210
Nikon Nikkormat FS	1966	160-200
Nikon Nikkormat FT	1966	120-150
Nikon Nikkormat FT, black	1966	1480-1700
Nikon Nikkormat FT2	1975	190-220
Nikon Nikkormat FT2, black	1975	200-250
Nikon Nikkormat FT3	1977	150-200
Nikon Nikkormat FT3, black	1977	130-170
Nikon Nikkormat FTn	1967	130-175
Nikon Nikkormat FTn, black	1967	180-210
Nikon Nikonos III	1975	280-320
Nikon Nikonos IVa	1980	200-240
Nikon Nikonos RS (sub)	1992	750-850
Nikon Nikonos RS AF	1992	1800-2200
Nikon Nikonos V	1983	350-450
Nikon Pronea 600i (Aps)	1996	250-300
Nikon Pronea S (Aps)	1998	40-65
Nikon S	1951	1800-2200
Nikon S MIOJ	1951	2000-2500
Nikon S2, chrome	1954	700-850

Manufacturer-model	Year	€
Nikon S2, black	1954	10000-12000*
Nikon S2-E, black	1954	50000-55000*
Nikon S3 2000 Millenium	2000	2000-2450
Nikon S3 M	1960	28000-32000*
Nikon S3, chrome	1958	1600-2000
Nikon S3, black	1958	2900-3400
Nikon S3, Olympic	1964	10000-12000*
Nikon S4 chrome	1959	2000-2450
Nikon SP, chrome	1957	1900-2200
Nikon SP, black	1957	5800-6500*

Noblex

Manufacturer-model	Year	€
Noblex 135U	1997	500-650
Noblex 135U	1997	1100-1400
Noblex PRO 06/150	1993	1300-1550
Noblex PRO 06/150E	1996	2100-2250
Noblex PRO 06/150U	1993	1400-1550
Noblex PRO 06/150UX	1998	2300-2600
Noblex PRO 175	1997	2200-2450

Officine Galileo

Manufacturer-model	Year	€
Condor	1957	400-450
Condor Avigo	----	550-650
Condor Ferrania	1951	140-160
Condor I	1947	180-220
Condor II	1953	300-350
Condorette Ferrania	----	70-100

Olympus

Manufacturer-model	Year	€
Olympus 35 DC	----	80-100
Olympus 35SP	----	125-140
Olympus AZ 4	1989	55-65
Olympus C-740	----	65-90
Olympus Camedia C-120	2002	25-35
Olympus Camedia C-2000	----	25-40
Olympus Camedia C-750	----	40-60
Olympus Camedia D-630	----	40-60
Olympus Camedia E-20N	----	120-140
Olympus Centurion	1996	25-40

Manufacturer-model	Year	€
Olympus EC2	----	50-70
Olympus ECRU	----	140-155
Olympus E-PL5	----	250-300
Olympus FE-190	----	30-40
Olympus FE-310	----	30-40
Olympus FE-370	----	35-45
Olympus FE-4000	----	35-45
Olympus FE-4020	----	50-65
Olympus FTL	1971	125-140
Olympus IS 100	1996	25-40
Olympus IS 1000	1990	25-40
Olympus IS 2000	1992	25-40
Olympus IS 300	1999	25-40
Olympus IS 3000	1992	55-65
Olympus IS 500	2002	25-40
Olympus IS 5000 QD	2002	40-60
Olympus M1	1972	450-550
Olympus M1 nera	1972	1.000-
Olympus Mju2	----	140-160
Olympus OM 1	1972	100-120
Olympus OM 10	1979	45-55
Olympus OM 10 Quartz	1980	45-55
Olympus OM 101	1988	40-60
Olympus OM 1N	1979	140-160
Olympus OM 2	1975	80-100

Manufacturer-model	Year	€
Olympus OM 2 black	1979	100-120
Olympus OM 2 Spot Program	1984	155-170
Olympus OM 20	1982	55-65
Olympus OM 3	1983	300-400
Olympus OM 3 Ti	1995	45-550
Olympus OM 30	1982	55-65
Olympus OM 4	1983	300-350
Olympus OM 4 Ti	1985	400-450
Olympus OM 40	1985	70-90
Olympus OM 707	1986	40-60
Olympus OM-1	1972	120-140
Olympus OM-1 (chrome)	----	120-150
Olympus OM-1 MD	1974	90-110
Olympus OM-1 black	1972	190-220
Olympus OM-10	1979	70-90
Olympus OM-10 FC	1982	50-70
Olympus OM-10 Quartz	1980	50-70
Olympus OM-101	1988	30-50
Olympus OM-1n	1979	120-140
Olympus OM-1n, black	1979	170-190
Olympus OM-2 MD	1975	140-160
Olympus OM-2 MD black	1975	200-220
Olympus OM-20	1982	40-60
Olympus OM-2000	1997	40-60
Olympus OM-2n	1979	140-160

Manufacturer-model	Year	€
Olympus OM-2n, black	1979	160-180
Olympus OM-2SP	1984	130-150
Olympus OM-3, black	1983	350-400
Olympus OM-30	1982	50-70
Olympus OM-3Ti	1985	900-1200
Olympus OM-4	1983	200-270
Olympus OM-40 Program	1985	90-110
Olympus OM-4Ti	1985	400-450
Olympus OM-707AF	1986	30-50
Olympus OM-D E-M1	----	400-500
Olympus OM-D E-M5	----	250-300
Olympus Pen EE-3	----	70-85
Olympus Pen F	1963	230-260
Olympus Pen F (18X24 mm)	1963	150-180
Olympus Pen F SLR	----	50-65
Olympus Pen FT	1966	290-320
Olympus Pen FT black	1966	390-420
Olympus Pen FTL (18X24	1970	170-200
Olympus Pen FV	1967	220-250
Olympus Pen FV black	1967	600-650
Olympus Trip 35	----	40-50
Olympus XA	----	45-60
Olympus XA2	----	65-75
Olympus XA-4	----	150-170

Pentacon

Manufacturer-model	Year	€
Pentacon	1948	190-225
Pentacon "no name"	1948	500-600
Pentacon E	1956	100-140
Pentacon F	1957	60-95
Pentacon FBM	1957	190-220
Pentacon FM	1957	140-165
Pentacon Six TL	1962	150-175
Pentacon Super	1966	250-300

Pentax

Manufacturer-model	Year	€
Asahi Pentax 6X7 TTL	----	485-560
Pentax 645N	----	500-600
Pentax A 3	1985	100-120
Pentax Auto-110 Mini	----	85-100
Pentax Efina T APS	----	25-35
Pentax Espio 140V	----	30-45
Pentax Espio 160	----	25-35
Pentax IQ	----	18-30
Pentax IQ Zoom 105G	----	20-35

Manufacturer-model	Year	€
Pentax IQ Zoom 105G	----	28-40
Pentax IQ Zoom 115S	----	22-44
Pentax IQ Zoom 130M	----	20-35
Pentax IQ Zoom 140	----	20-40
Pentax IQ Zoom 140M	----	60-75
Pentax IQ Zoom 160	----	20-35
Pentax IQ Zoom 200 QD Date	----	28-40
Pentax IQ Zoom 80S	----	25-35
Pentax IQ Zoom 90MC	----	25-35
Pentax IQ Zoom EZY-R	----	25-35
Pentax IQZoom 105SW	----	30-45
Pentax IQZoom 120SW	----	22-38
Pentax IQZoom 170SL	----	170-210
Pentax IQZoom 170SL	----	20-35
Pentax IQZoom 60S	----	25-40
Pentax IQZoom 90WR	----	25-40
Pentax IQZoom 928	----	40-55
Pentax IQZoom EZY-80	----	18-28
Pentax K 1000	1977	100-125
Pentax K 2	1975	160-180
Pentax K 2 DMD	1976	160-185
Pentax KM	1975	100-125
Pentax KX	1975	130-150
Pentax LX	1980	250-300
Pentax ME	1976	70-90

Manufacturer-model	Year	€
Pentax ME Super	1980	70-90
Pentax ME-F	1981	80-100
Pentax MG	1982	80-95
Pentax MV	1980	70-90
Pentax MV 1	1980	70-90
Pentax MX	1976	120-140
Pentax MZ 10	1996	120-145
Pentax MZ 3	1997	120-150
Pentax MZ 30	1900	140-165
Pentax MZ 5	1996	120-150
Pentax MZ 50	1997	140-170
Pentax MZ 5-N	1998	120-145
Pentax MZ 7	1999	140-165
Pentax MZ M	1997	120-140
Pentax P 30	1985	60-85
Pentax P 30 N	1989	60-80
Pentax P 30 T	1991	60-85
Pentax P 50	1986	70-95
Pentax P3	----	100-120
Pentax P30T	----	80-110
Pentax P3n	----	80-95
Pentax PC-330	----	50-70
Pentax Program A	1984	80-100
Pentax PZ-10	----	70-90
Pentax PZ-20	----	100-150

Manufacturer-model	Year	€
Pentax PZ70	----	45-60
Pentax SF 7	1988	90-110
Pentax SF X	1987	100-120
Pentax SF X-N	1988	110-140
Pentax SF10	----	70-85
Pentax Super A	1983	100-125
Pentax Super Program	----	70-85
Pentax Z 1	1992	150-170
Pentax Z 10	1991	100-125
Pentax Z 1-P	1994	200-230
Pentax Z 20	1992	100-125
Pentax Z 50-P	1993	100-130
Pentax Z 70	1994	100-140
Pentax Zoom 105-R	----	15-25
Pentax Zoom 70-r	----	25-40
Pentax Zx-10	----	40-60
Pentax ZX-30	----	80-100
Pentax ZX-5 SLR	----	150-200
Pentax ZX-50	----	30-45
Pentax ZX-5N	----	100-120
Pentax ZX-7	----	80-100
Pentax ZX-L Date AF SLR	----	90-120
Pentax ZX-M	----	100-120

Petri

Manufacturer-model	Year	€
Petri 7	----	80-100
Petri FA-1	1975	50-70
Petri Flex V	1965	40-60
Petri FT	1967	50-70
Petri FT EE	1970	50-65
Petri FT II	1970	50-65
Petri FTE	1975	40-60
Petri MF 101	1976	20-40
Petri MF 4	1979	30-50
Petri MF-1	1977	50-70
Petri MF-103	1981	40-60
Petri MF-104	1981	40-60
Petri MF-2	1979	50-70
Petri MF-3	1980	40-65
Petri MF-4	1980	40-65
Petri Penta V2	1960	90-110
Petri TTL	1974	40-60
Petri TTL 2	1979	40-60

Plaubel - Makina

Manufacturer-model	Year	€
Plaubel Makina 6X7	----	1500-1750
Plaubel Makina Mod 1	1920-1933	400-600
Plaubel Makina W67	----	1500-1650
Plaubel Monorail 4X5	----	800-1000
Plaubel Monorail 8X10	----	2200-2450
Plaubel Telemeter	----	280-340
Plaubel W69 Proshit	----	1800-2400

Polaroid

Manufacturer-model	Year	€
Polaroid 103	----	75-95
Polaroid 210 Automatic	----	20-40
Polaroid 2100	----	18-25
Polaroid 220 land	----	40-60
Polaroid 320 Instant Pack	----	35-48
Polaroid 635 CL	----	70-85
Polaroid 645	----	50-60
Polaroid colorpack 88	1971	25-40
Polaroid Hunter Green OneStep	----	25-40
Polaroid Instant 1000 de luxe	1978	70-90
Polaroid Land	----	50-70
Polaroid Modello 20 Land	1965	70-90
Polaroid One 600 Ultra Instant	----	40-60
Polaroid One Step Flash	----	55-80
Polaroid PIC-300 Instant Film	----	40-60
Polaroid ProPack Professional	----	27-45
Polaroid Scrapbook Photo Album	----	18-28
Polaroid Spectra System SE	----	35-45
Polaroid Spirit 600 CL	----	50-70
Polaroid Super Shooter Plus	----	15-25
Polaroid Supercolor 635CL	----	45-60
Polaroid SX-70 The Button	----	25-40
Polaroid Ultrapack	----	50-70

Praktica

Manufacturer-model	Year	€
Hanimex Praktica 66	----	120-140
Hanimex Praktica Super TL	----	25-55
Praktica 66 Waist	----	40-60
Praktica 66 Waist	----	240-280
Praktica 66 Waist	----	35-60
Praktica B 100	1980	50-65
Praktica B 200	1981	40-60
Praktica B200 Electronic	----	35-60
Praktica B200S	----	800-1000
Praktica BC 1	1984	40-60
Praktica BC-A	1986	50-70
Praktica BCA Electronic	----	40-60
Praktica BMS	1989	40-60
Praktica BX 20	1989	50-65
Praktica BX 20-S	1990	80-100
Praktica EE 2	1977	50-65
Praktica FX2	----	150-200
Praktica IV	----	35-45
Praktica IV FB	----	100-120
Praktica L	----	40-55
Praktica L 2	1976	40-60
Praktica L3-ENDO	----	50-70
Praktica LB 2	1976	40-60
Praktica LB2 PORST CX4	----	30-42
Praktica L-Endoskopie	----	120-140
Praktica LLC	1969	40-60
Praktica LTL 2	----	70-95
Praktica LTL 3	1976	50-70
Praktica model FX3	----	40-60
Praktica MTL 3	1979	30-45

Manufacturer-model	Year	€
Praktica MTL 5	----	28-45
Praktica MTL 50	1985	30-45
Praktica MTL 5b	1984	40-60
Praktica Nova E	----	20-40
Praktica PLC 2	1976	30-50
Praktica PLC 3	1979	40-60
Praktica Super TL 3	1978	50-70
Praktica Super TL-2 SLR	----	25-55
Praktica VLC	1975	60-80
Praktica VLC 2	1976	60-80
Praktica VLC 3	1978	60-80
Praktiflex FX	----	28-42
Praktisix	1957	150-180

Rectaflex

Manufacturer-model	Year	€
Rectaflex 40000 Roma	1956	4000-5000
Rectaflex Junior	1950	650-750
Rectaflex Junior	1951	700-850
Rectaflex Liechtenstein	1956	4000-5000
Rectaflex Rotor	1952	2500-2800
Rectaflex Standard	1952	2000-2500
Rectaflex Standard A.1000	1949	800-1000
Rectaflex Standard B 16000	1951	700-850
Rectaflex Standard B 2000	1949	700-850
Rectaflex Standard B 3000	1949	700-900
Rectaflex Standard B 4000	1950	1200-1450
Regula Reflex 2000 CTL	1970	150-200

Revueflex

Manufacturer-model	Year	€
Revueflex 1001	1976	30-45
Revueflex 2002	1976	30-50
Revueflex 3003	1976	30-40
Revueflex 4004	1976	30-45
Revueflex 5000EE	1976	30-50
Revueflex 5005	1976	30-55
Revueflex AC1	1978	30-55

Ricoh

Manufacturer-model	Year	€
Ricoh 35 V Auto	----	45-55
Ricoh 35FM	----	20-35
Ricoh 500G	----	70-80
Ricoh Auto 66	----	90-110
Ricoh Auto Half E 25	----	15-25
Ricoh Auto Half SE	----	35-40
Ricoh Auto TLS EE	1976	50-65
Ricoh Caddy half frame	1960	85-100
Ricoh Caplio GX200	----	40-60
Ricoh CR-5	----	40-50

Manufacturer-model	Year	€
Ricoh DC-2E	----	20-30
Ricoh FF 90 Auto Focus		18-28
Ricoh FF1	----	55-75
Ricoh FF-1	----	55-75
Ricoh FF-9D	----	20-40
Ricoh Five One Nine	----	800-1000
Ricoh Flex Model VII	----	80-100
Ricoh GR Digital II	----	150-170
Ricoh GR10 Black	----	320-360
Ricoh GR1s	----	370-400
Ricoh GR1v	----	450-550
Ricoh GR21	----	800-1000
Ricoh GX200 Digital	----	70-100
Ricoh GXR S10	----	140-160
Ricoh Hi-Color	----	55-65
Ricoh KR 10	1980	80-100
Ricoh KR 10 M	1991	70-90
Ricoh KR 10 Super	1983	40-50
Ricoh KR 10-X	1988	30-40
Ricoh KR 30sp	----	65-85
Ricoh KR 5	1980	30-40
Ricoh KR 5 Super	1983	30-40
Ricoh KR 5 Super II	1989	40-50
Ricoh KR10M	1991	30-40
Ricoh KR10X	1988	60-70

Manufacturer-model	Year	€
Ricoh KR30SP	----	25-40
Ricoh KR5	----	140-160
Ricoh KR5 Super	1983	30-40
Ricoh KR5 Super II	1989	40-50
Ricoh KSX	----	25-45
Ricoh LX-33 W AF	----	35-45
Ricoh Mirai	1988	30-40
Ricoh MY-1	----	60-70
Ricoh Pentax Q-S1	----	160-180
Ricoh Q-80Z	----	20-30
Ricoh R1	----	60-80
Ricoh R1S	----	65-75
Ricoh R1s	----	120-145
Ricoh RDC-300Z	----	55-70
Ricoh Ricohmatic 126	----	35-45
Ricoh Ricohmatic 44	----	90-100
Ricoh RT 550	----	45-55
Ricoh RZ-1000	----	55-70
Ricoh S-2	----	140-160
Ricoh See-Thru transparent	----	140-170
Ricoh Shotmaster	----	25-40
Ricoh Singlex	1964	100-120
Ricoh Singlex TLS	----	120-170
Ricoh Singlex TLS	1968	60-75
Ricoh SLX 500	1975	40-55

Manufacturer-model	Year	€
Ricoh Super Ricohfle	----	80-90
Ricoh Theta S	----	180-220
Ricoh TLS 401	1970	70-80
Ricoh TLS EE	1973	50-60
Ricoh WG-20	----	70-100
Ricoh WG-30 Red (red)	----	240-280
Ricoh WG-M1 waterproof	----	120-150
Ricoh XR 1	1977	40-50
Ricoh XR 2	1978	40-50
Ricoh XR 20 SP	1985	50-65
Ricoh XR 500	1980	40-55
Ricoh XR 6	1980	30-45
Ricoh XR 7	1981	50-60
Ricoh XR 7MII	----	40-65
Ricoh XR M	1983	50-60
Ricoh XR P	1984	80-90
Ricoh XR S (solar cells)	1981	100-120
Ricoh XR Solar	1995	90-110
Ricoh XR X	1987	80-100
Ricoh XR X 3-PF	1994	70-90
Ricoh XR X-3000	1997	70-90
Ricoh XR2S	1978	70-90
Ricoh XR7 autofocus	1981	60-75
Ricoh XRF	1984	90-100
Ricoh XRS	1982	100-120
Ricoh XR-S Solar	1995	90-110
Ricoh YF-20	----	20-30
Ricoh YF-20D	----	65-80

Robot

Manufacturer-model	Year	€
Robot Recorder 24	----	190-260
Robot	1930	400-500
Robot II	----	120-16
Robot IIa Prototipo	----	1000-1400
Robot Junior	----	260-300
Robot l	----	550-650
Robot Royal MOD III	----	500-600
Robot Star 50	----	1000-1250
Robot Vollautomat Star II	----	140-180

Rollei

Manufacturer-model	Year	€
Rollei 16 Miniature Spy	----	100-125
Rollei 16 S	----	65-75
Rollei 35	----	220-260
Rollei 35 Classic	----	1000-1400
Rollei 35 Gold (gold)	----	850-1000
Rollei 35 Led	----	65-75
Rollei 35 Platin	----	1400-1600
Rollei 35 S	----	300-400
Rollei 35 TE Black	----	50-65

Manufacturer-model	Year	€
Rollei 35RF Chrome	----	900-1000
Rollei 35SE	----	500-600
Rollei 6008 Integral	----	1400-1600
Rollei A 110	----	60-80
Rollei A26	----	20-35
Rollei AFM 35	----	460-520
Rollei B 35	----	55-65
Rollei C35	----	140-180
Rollei Prego	----	55-65
Rollei QZ 35T	----	400-500
Rollei SL 2000 F + back	1981	200-250
Rollei SL 3001 + back	1986	300-350
Rollei SL 3003 + back	1984	350-400
Rollei SL 35 (Germany)	1972	130-160
Rollei SL 35 (Singapore)	1972	70-90
Rollei SL 35 E	1976	120-140
Rollei SL 35 M	1976	60-80
Rollei SL 35 MF	1976	120-140
Rollei SL 350	1974	200-220
Rollei X115	----	75-100
Rollei XF 35	----	55-75
Rolleicord I	1933	190-210
Rolleicord I	1934	100-120
Rolleicord II	1936	100-120
Rolleicord IId	1936	100-120

Manufacturer-model	Year	€
Rolleicord III	----	250-320
Rolleicord V	----	400-500
Rolleicord Va	1957	180-200
Rolleicord Vb	1962	250-270
Rolleiflex 2,8 GX	1987	1200-1400
Rolleiflex 2,8F Aurum	1983	1850-2200
Rolleiflex 2,8F Planar	1960	1200-1400
Rolleiflex 2,8F Platinum	1984	2500-2700
Rolleiflex 2,8F Xenotar	1963	750-900
Rolleiflex 2.8 E	----	1400-1600
Rolleiflex 3,5F xenotar	1959	500-600
Rolleiflex 3.5F Planar	1959	700-800
Rolleiflex 3001	1986	350-450
Rolleiflex 3003	1985	650-750
Rolleiflex 35 E	----	400-500
Rolleiflex 4X4 Baby, nera	1963	450-550
Rolleiflex 6001 Professional	1999	2000-2500
Rolleiflex 6002	1986	600-750
Rolleiflex 6003 Professional	1996	1300-1500
Rolleiflex 6006	1984	500-650
Rolleiflex 6006/2	1987	1100-1300
Rolleiflex 6008 Integral	1996	1000-1200
Rolleiflex 6008 Professional	1988	1750-2000
Rolleiflex Automat MX	----	300-400
Rolleiflex Baby 4x4	----	180-240

Manufacturer-model	Year	€
Rolleiflex wide-angle lens	1961	2200-2400
Rolleiflex Magic I	1960	260-290
Rolleiflex SL 66	1966	450-550
Rolleiflex SL 66E	1982	1000-1200
Rolleiflex SL 66E Excl. Pro	1992	2500-2700
Rolleiflex SL2000 F	1980	300-350
Rolleiflex SL35 E	1978	160-180
Rolleiflex SL35 M	1976	70-90
Rolleiflex SL35 ME	1976	60-80
Rolleiflex SL35, Germany	1972	100-120
Rolleiflex SL35, Singapore	1972	60-80
Rolleiflex SL350	1974	100-120
Rolleiflex SLX	1974	350-370
Rolleiflex T Tessar	1958	300-320
Rolleiflex T Xenar	1975	350-370
Rolleiflex Tele	1959	1100-1200
Rolleimagic II	1962	220-260

Seagull

Manufacturer-model	Year	€
Seagull 203	----	75-100
Seagull 4A SA-85	----	140-160
Seagull 4A TLR 6x6	----	75-90
Seagull 4B-1 Twin	----	120-140
Seagull DF 1	1969	30-50
Seagull DF 300	1985	40-60
Seagull DF 300 X	1994	40-60
Seagull Twin 4	----	220-240

Sealife

Manufacturer-model	Year	€
Sealife DC 1400	----	150-185
Sealife DC 600	----	20-30
Sealife DC1200	----	350-450
Sealife DC500	----	160-180
Sealife DC800	----	20-25
Sealife Reefmaster CL	----	55-75
Sealife Reefmaster PRO SL560	----	90-100
Sealife Reefmaster SL201	----	25-40
SeaLife SL-100	----	20-25
SeaLife SportDiver	----	25-40
Sealift 35 Reefmaster	----	25-35

Sears

Manufacturer-model	Year	€
Sears 65	----	95-110
Sears Tls Chrome	----	85-100
Sears Tower 51	----	90-110
Sears Tower 55 B	----	29-45
Sears Tower 57-A	----	88-95
Sears Tower One-Twenty Flash	----	50-65
Sears Trumpfreflex	----	70-90
Sears KSX 1000	----	40-55
Sears SL11 Chrome	----	25-40
Sears KS 500	----	70-90

Taisei

Manufacturer-model	Year	€
Taisei Koki Super Westomat 35	----	85-100
Taisei Koki Welmy Six L	----	45-60
Taisei Koki Welmy Six Model E	----	45-65
Taisei Koki Westomat 35	----	80-100
Taisei Welmy Six Model E	----	55-70
Taisei Welmy Six W	----	50-70

Topcon

Manufacturer-model	Year	€
Topcon	1978	60-80
Topcon Auto 100	----	250-380
Topcon Horseman 970	----	220-280
Topcon Horseman Press	----	240-280
Topcon Horseman VH-R	----	280-330
Topcon IC-1 Auto	----	140-170
Topcon R	----	150-200
Topcon RE 2	1965	160-180
Topcon RE 200	1977	50-70
Topcon RE 300	1978	50-70
Topcon RE Super	1963	230-260

Manufacturer-model	Year	€
Topcon RM 300	1977	50-70
Topcon Sawyer's Mark IV	----	250-280
Topcon Super D	1972	180-210
Topcon Super DM	1973	250-280
Topcon Uni	1964	40-65
Topcon Unirex	1969	40-65
Topcon Unirex EE	1975	50-70
Topcon, Hanimex RE 2 SLR	----	90-110

Tower

Manufacturer-model	Year	€
Tower 10	----	45-60
Tower 20 B	----	55-70
Tower 35 mm	----	29-40
Tower 37 a	----	50-70
Tower 39 Automatic	----	28-55
Tower 55 B	----	55-70
Tower 57 a	----	100-120
Tower Folding Pocket 120-	----	50-65
Tower Formato 120 metallo	1930*	50-70
Tower Model B	----	45-60
Tower Model Flash Automatic	----	40-55
Tower Snappy	----	45-60

Voigtländer

Manufacturer-model	Year	€
Voigtlander Bessa	1937	55-70
Voigtlander Bessa I	----	95-110
Voigtländer Bessamatic	1959	280-310
Voigtländer Bessamatic	1962	70-90
Voigtländer Bessamatic CS	1967	150-180
Voigtlander Box	----	50-70
Voigtlander Brillant	1932	100-120
Voigtländer Ultramatic	1962	90-110
Voigtländer Ultramatic CS	1963	130-150
Voigtländer Vito	1947	70-90
Voigtländer Vito C	1967	65-80
Voigtländer Vito II	1949	90-110
Voigtländer Vitoret DR	1964	70-90
Voigtländer Vitoret LR	1967	60-80
Voigtländer VSL 1 (Germ)	1974	60-80
Voigtlander VSL 1 (Sing)	1975	40-60
Voigtlander VSL 2	1976	60-80
Voigtlander VSL 3 E	1979	50-70
Voigtländer VSL1 BM	1975	50-70

Walz

Manufacturer-model	Year	€
Walz Electric	----	95-120
Walz Envoy 35	----	100-125
Walz Walzflex	----	70-95

Wirgin

Manufacturer-model	Year	€
Wirgin Edina	----	72-90
Wirgin Edixa	----	82-100
Wirgin Edixa Flex	----	95-115
Wirgin Edixa Ii	----	83-95
Wirgin Stereo	----	100-115

Yashica

Manufacturer-model	Year	€
Yashica 106	1996	40-55
Yashica 107 MP	1988	40-60
Yashica 108 MP	1989	50-70
Yashica 109 MP	1995	70-90

Manufacturer-model	Year	€
Yashica 124 G	1970	150-180
Yashica 200 AF	1987	40-60
Yashica 230 AF	1987	30-50
Yashica 270 AF	1992	60-80
Yashica 300 AF	1993	70-90
Yashica D	1958	60-80
Yashica Dental Eye	1985	400-450
Yashica Electro 35 G	1966	80-100
Yashica Electro 35 GS	1970	70-90
Yashica Electro 35 GSN	1973	70-95
Yashica Electro 35 GT black	1969	80-110
Yashica Electro 35 GTN	1973	80-100
Yashica FR	1976	30-50
Yashica FR I	1978	60-80
Yashica FR-II	1978	40-60
Yashica FX 1	1975	40-60
Yashica FX 103	1985	50-70
Yashica FX 2	1977	30-45
Yashica FX 3	1980	40-60
Yashica FX 3 Super	1984	50-70
Yashica FX 3 Super 2000	1986	60-80
Yashica FX 70	1984	40-60
Yashica FX103 P	1985	60-80
Yashica FX3 2000 Super	1986	70-90
Yashica FX-D Quartz	1981	50-70

Manufacturer-model	Year	€
Yashica Mat 124	1968	130-150
Yashica Pentamatic	1960	110-130
Yashica Samurai x3	1987	40-60
Yashica Samurai x4	1988	40-65
Yashica Samurai Z	1989	90-115
Yashica Samurai ZL	1989	180-210
Yashica T3	----	50-70
Yashica T3 Super	----	50-70
Yashica T4	----	120-145
Yashica T4 Safari edition	----	120-150
Yashica T4 Super	----	120-140
Yashica T5	----	150-180
Yashica TL Electro	1975	50-70
Yashica TL Electro AX	1973	40-60
Yashica TL Electro X	1970	70-90
Yashica TL Electro X ITS	1975	50-70
Yashica TL Super	1967	40-60
Yashica YE	1959	350-390
Yashica YF	1959	280-320

Zeiss

Manufacturer-model	Year	€
Zeiss Contessa 35	----	160-185
Zeiss Icarette	----	22-50
Zeiss Ikoflex Favorit	----	240-300
Zeiss Ikoflex I	----	120-170
Zeiss Ikon	2004	450-500
Zeiss Ikon Contaflex Super	1964	110-135
Zeiss Ikon Contaflex Super BC	1965	140-170
Zeiss Ikon Contarex I "Ciclope"	1959	500-600
Zeiss Ikon Contarex Prof	1966	900-1000
Zeiss Ikon Contarex Special	1960	700-900
Zeiss Ikon Contarex Super	1967	800-1000
Zeiss Ikon Contarex Super II	1969	850-1100
Zeiss Ikon Icarex 35 BM	1968	70-90
Zeiss Ikon Icarex 35 TM	1969	70-90
Zeiss Ikon Icarex 35-S BM	1968	80-110
Zeiss Ikon Icarex 35-S TM	1969	80-100
Zeiss Ikon SL 706	1971	2500-3000
Zeiss Ikon SL 706	1972	170-195
Zeiss Ikonta 35	----	45-65
Zeiss Ikonta A 521	----	4570
Zeiss Miroflex B	----	350-400

Zenit

Manufacturer-model	Year	€
Zenit	1952	350-400
Zenit	1953	450-500
Zenit 11	1983	20-45
Zenit 12 XP	1984	40-60
Zenit 122	----	85-110
Zenit 122	1990	40-60
Zenit 12CD	----	80-100
Zenit 19	1979	40-60
Zenit 212 K	1995	40-60
Zenit 22	1980	40-60
Zenit 3	1962	50-75
Zenit 312 K	2000	40-60
Zenit -3M	----	70-90
Zenit Auto	----	86-100
Zenit B	1968	30-45
Zenit E	1966	40-55
Zenit EM	1973	50-70
Zenit -ET	----	70-90
Zenit Sniper (photographic gun)	1988	150-180
Zenit T1	1979	40-60
Zenit TTL	1975	50-70
Zenit-E Olympic 80	----	70-90

Zenza Bronica

Manufacturer-model	Year	€
Zenza Bronica C2	1965	210-250
Zenza Bronica D	1959	600-750
Zenza Bronica EC	1972	220-280
Zenza Bronica EC-TL	1976	350-400
Zenza Bronica ETR	1976	250-300
Zenza Bronica ETR-C	1978	320-400
Zenza Bronica ETR-S	1980	360-410
Zenza Bronica ETR-Si	1989	160-195
Zenza Bronica GS-1	1983	400-455
Zenza Bronica RF645	2000	800-885
Zenza Bronica S	1961	200-240
Zenza Bronica S2	1965	260-300
Zenza Bronica S2 A	1971	400-445
Zenza Bronica SQ	1981	280-325
Zenza Bronica SQ-A	1982	160-190
Zenza Bronica SQ-Ai	1990	400-440
Zenza Bronica SQ-AM	1982	160-190
Zenza Bronica SQ-B	1996	500-600

Zorki

Manufacturer-model	Year	€
Zorki 1	1948	70-95
Zorki 1 C	----	6085
Zorki 10	----	40-65
Zorki 11	----	50-75
Zorki 12	----	250-285
Zorki 2	1954	120-155
Zorki 2 C	----	90-115
Zorki 2 S	----	50-70
Zorki 3	1951	60-80
Zorki 3 C	----	80-100
Zorki 3 M	----	140-160
Zorki 4 K	1956	120-145
Zorki 5	----	50-70
Zorki 6	----	45-65
Zorki C	----	45-70
Zorki KMZ	----	80-100

Books published by the author

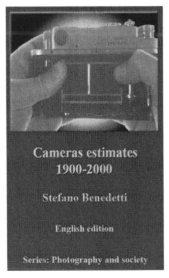

Camera lenses estimates
Stefano Benedetti

International edition
Series photography and society

Painting on the screen

Stefano Benedetti

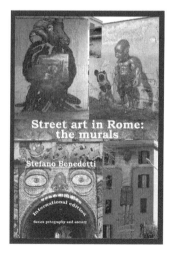

Street art in Rome:
the murals

Stefano Benedetti

International edition

Series petography and society

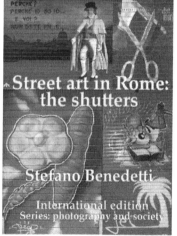

Street art in Rome:
the shutters

Stefano Benedetti

International edition
Series: photography and society

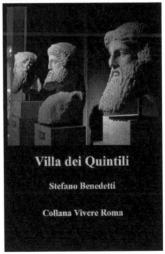

La valle della Caffarella

Stefano Benedetti

Collana Vivere Roma

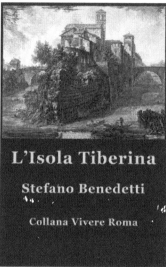

L'Isola Tiberina

Stefano Benedetti

Collana Vivere Roma

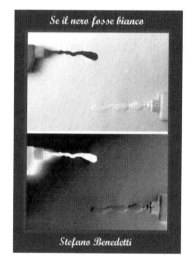

Se il nero fosse bianco

Stefano Benedetti

Fiabe per adulti
Stefano Benedetti
Seconda edizione

148

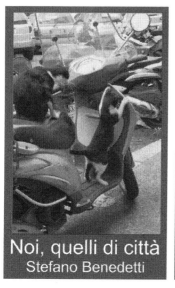

Noi, quelli di città
Stefano Benedetti

Allium, cioè proprietà farmacologiche, storia, coltivazione, ricette e benefici dell'aglio

Stefano Benedetti

Collana: Alimentazione e benessere

Allium Cepa
cioè tutto quello che è utile sapere sulla cipolla

Stefano Benedetti

Collana: Alimentazione e benessere

Juglans Regia, cioè la ghianda di Giove più importante: la noce

Stefano Benedetti

Collana Alimentazione e benessere

Malus domestica, cioè il pomo della conoscenza: la mela

Stefano Benedetti

Collana Alimentazione e benessere

KRENF

STEFANO BENEDETTI

Briciole di terra

Fra prosa, poesia e canzone

Stefano Benedetti

Poesie proibite

Stefano Benedetti

Fotografia caleidoscopica

Stefano Benedetti

Collana Fotografia e società

Ritratti

poesie matematiche

Stefano Benedetti

Le quotazioni di 2200
apparecchi fotografici
dal 1900 al 2000

Stefano Benedetti

Collana Fotografia e società

Le stime degli obiettivi fotografici

Stefano Benedetti

Collana fotografia e società

Le stime delle fotocamere
Edizione 2017-2018

Stefano Benedetti

Collana Fotografia e società

Le stime degli obiettivi
Edizione 2017-2018

Stefano Benedetti

Collana Fotografia e società

Il magico numero nove
e i suoi amici multipli

Stefano Benedetti

Books distribution

Paper Version: Createspace – Il miolibro

Ebook: Amazon – Kobo- Ilmiolibro

And

All national and international stores

26456657R00085

Printed in Great Britain
by Amazon